He Calls Me
His Child

100 Days of Meditations
on the Promises of God

MARIE CHAPIAN

BroadStreet
PUBLISHING

BroadStreet Publishing® Group, LLC
Savage, Minnesota, USA
BroadStreetPublishing.com

He Calls Me His Child: 100 Days of Meditations on the Promises of God
Copyright © 2024 Marie Chapian

9781424567201 (faux leather)
9781424567218 (ebook)

Stock or custom editions of BroadStreet Publishing titles may be purchased in bulk for educational, business, ministry, fundraising, or sales promotional use. For information, please email orders@broadstreetpublishing.com

Cover and interior by Garborg Design Works | garborgdesign.com

Printed in China

24 25 26 27 28 5 4 3 2 1

HOW TO READ THIS BOOK

I've written this book as a thoughtful practice of God's Word for a deeper reality of our identity and power as children of God. *He Calls Me His Child* is a call to awareness and action. How are we to live the sacred position we hold in the kingdom of God in this time? The one hundred meditations in this book point to the power and authority God has given us to live bold, overcoming lives at all times.

Jesus explained his presence to the world as coming from heaven to earth for the express purpose of showing us the heart, mind, and soul of God in every word he proclaimed, in every miracle he performed, and in everything he did. Jesus is our role model for how to speak, affirm, and live the truth that glorifies the Lord.

In my previous books on Quiet Prayer Christian meditation, I defined meditation as dedicated periods of silence with God. The meditations here are words to read for insight into the nature of God and our human nature and to gain spiritual wisdom to be transformed into his image (2 Corinthians 3:18). The meditations prepare us for the affirmations that follow. Pause to think about what you've read and then go on with intention and purpose as you speak the affirmations. Based on the promises of God in his written Word, they are profound statements of spiritual power. Every affirmation in this book is a true, Holy Spirit–filled statement founded on the redemptive work of Christ and the ratified fact of the new covenant in his blood.

But why affirmations? Our daily self-talk is often in direct opposition to the blessings, gifts, and purpose of the Lord. We don't realize how affected our brains are by negative self-talk like, "God never talks to me." Can that be true? Jesus said in John 10:27, "My sheep hear My voice, and I know them, and they follow Me." We wonder why we're depressed, tired, bored, anxious, fearful. It's because we're not speaking the truth to ourselves. "Death and life are in the power of the tongue" (Proverbs 18:21). The next time we speak out of turn, are rude or self-effacing, we need to do a mouth checkup. What's in our words? Life or death? Now is a good time to partner with the Holy Spirit and stop speaking and repeating negative, life-swallowing lies that contradict God's truth.

Jesus made affirmations all the time by proclaiming who he was and how he and the Father are one (John 10:30). He could do nothing without his Father. He said, "Most assuredly, I say to you, the Son can do nothing of Himself, but what He sees the Father do; for whatever He does, the Son also does in like manner" (5:19).

The Holy Spirit has taken permanent residence in you and will ignite your faith and relationship with the Lord Jesus. The reality of God's Word has power in these affirmations because they're true and eternal. When you affirm, "I no longer criticize others," you're not asking God to help you stop criticizing others; you're stating as a fact that you no longer criticize others.

Speak the affirmations aloud, but if it's uncomfortable for you to speak aloud, write the words down in a special notebook or enter them into your mobile device where you can look back on what you've written and see more clearly the work God makes alive in you. The spiritual inner work you're doing is transforming.

Take your time but make a daily practice out of using this book. You have faith and trust in God within you. Think of a time when you were in a dangerous situation that you didn't think you were strong enough to handle. All looked hopeless. Imagine that you took a deep breath and repeated Ephesians 6:10 to yourself: "I am strong in the Lord and in his might" (author's paraphrase). Then you handled the situation brilliantly, and good came out of it. Where did your strength come from? Did God think, *Oh dear, where did I put his (her) strength? It's around here somewhere*, and then send you an angel with a strength care package? No. His strength was already within you by the power of the Holy Spirit. You called into action the strength of the Lord in you.

Biblical affirmations are not just positive statements that don't contain the authority of the Holy Spirit. They are a daily practice of affirming and proclaiming faith and deep trust in God. The words you speak glorify the Lord, and his Word never returns to him without results that glorify him (Isaiah 55:10–11). It's my prayer that your journey into the promises of God will go on for years to come. I pray this book will kindle a new flame in your faith and give you more insight and multiply your blessings. You're following Jesus' example and admonition to fearlessly confirm and affirm the truth that sets us free.

Love,

Marie

A NEW BEGINNING

If anyone is in Christ, he is a new creation;
old things have passed away;
behold, all things have become new.

2 CORINTHIANS 5:17

"I will give them one heart, and I will put a new spirit
within them, and take the stony heart out of their flesh,
and give them a heart of flesh."

EZEKIEL 11:19

"For you who revere my name, the sun of righteousness will
rise with healing in its rays. And you will go out and frolic
like well-fed calves."

MALACHI 4:2 NIV

Meditate

Every day can be a new beginning. Every day when you
wake up and greet a new morning, it's a new event. Don't
wait to discover and experience your new beginnings. They
don't show up only when you're starting a new job, moving
to a new place to live, or starting a new relationship.

Of course, we may not always feel ready to tackle
such opportunities. The obstacles to taking hold of a new
beginning are old habits that could include shame, doubt,
grief, fear, lack of faith, and ignorance of what's out there
for you in God's kingdom on earth.

Lamentations 3:22–23 reads, "The steadfast love of
the LORD never ceases, his mercies never come to an end;

they are new every morning" (NRSVUE). How can your day be new every morning? Your new beginning is that moment when you decide to rest completely in the Lord's hands.

Imagine a beautiful theater stage setting of a new opera. You're the star of this opera, and you're standing on stage with the curtain about to go up. Your voice is warmed up, you've rehearsed your arias, and now it's showtime. The great thing is that you can't do this on your own. You must have the blessing and anointing of God before you can sing a note. Lifting your head from the pillow is like the orchestra tuning up. The conductor is about to enter an orchestra pit. This is the biggest event of your life. The curtain goes up to God's grace. Yes, waking up in the morning to meet God's grace is the biggest event of your day. It's your new beginning.

Affirmations

- I no longer see my morning as anything but a great event.
- The Holy Spirit in me is alive, and his mercies are new every morning that I wake.
- I am living in my new beginning every day.
- I play an important role in God's opera, and he is the director and my song.

BLESSED CHILD OF GOD

May the one who comes in the name of the LORD be blessed.
We will pronounce blessings on you in the LORD's temple.
PSALM 118:26 NET

"We pronounce a blessing on you in the name of the LORD."
PSALM 129:8 NET

"'May the LORD bless you and protect you.
May the LORD smile on you and be gracious to you.
May the LORD show you his favor and give you his peace.'"
NUMBERS 6:24–26 NLT

Meditate

The beautiful benediction found in Numbers 6:24–26 is a good example of the meaning of the word *blessing*. Look at blessing from the Lord's standpoint, and you'll find it in this prayer that God spoke to Moses. It begins "May the LORD bless you" (NLT) and then goes on to tell us what that means. Everything in this prayer defines the word *blessing*: favor, kindness, support, protection, grace (unmerited favor), mercy, preference, approval, and, finally, peace.

When David exhorted himself to "bless the LORD, O my soul" (Psalm 103:2), he used the word *bless* to mean to exalt, praise, honor, worship, and express true heartfelt gratitude from the depth of his very soul.

Live in the arms of blessing the way God uses the word. You are blessed. You are favored, supported, protected, smiled upon; shown kindness, grace, mercy; and given peace. All this in one word: *blessed*.

Speak and affirm the divine favor you carry into the world with you.

Affirmations

- I end the cycle of finding negativity everywhere and always focus on God's blessing.
- I put an end to sabotaging the blessings of God by being spiritually blind to them.
- The first thing I do when I wake in the morning is thank God for my blessings (Ephesians 1:3).
- I'm surrounded by God's blessings.
- I find blessings in every hour of the day.
- By living my life as blessed, I bless the Lord.
- The blessings of God are my inheritance.
- I am a blessing to others.
- I live a blessed life.

SILENCE

Truly my soul silently waits for God.
PSALM 62:1

The LORD is in his holy temple;
let all the earth be silent before him.
HABAKKUK 2:20 NIV

Be still [silent] before the LORD.
PSALM 37:7 NIV

Meditate

You have the very same access to God the Father that Jesus had. After the inner noise has settled and you're comfortable in the silence, a jumble of thoughts will inevitably interrupt you. *What's for dinner tonight? Why hasn't so-and-so called? Did I lock the back door? We need a new car.*

Come back to stillness. Prayer in this stillness is a wordless, reliant opening of your soul to interact with the presence of God. We take "not my will, but thine, be done" (Luke 22:42 KJV) into this time of silence. I like to spend the first moments of prayer in silence as a prelude. I take those moments to settle down, catch my breath, relax my body, and listen for his presence. It may sound strange to listen for silence, but God is in the silence. John of the Cross, a sixteenth-century saint, put it, "Silence is the first language of God."

If you use silence to figure something out, think through a problem, go over your calendar, make plans, or eat lunch, that's okay, but silence is best when doing nothing, saying nothing, and putting your busy thoughts aside. The more acquainted you are with silence in prayer, the less attracted to busy thoughts you'll become and the less attracted to the thought itself you'll become. Silence doesn't need to entertain itself. Silence is fine being silent.

God has prepared a secret place for you to rest, and it's alone with him in the silence (Psalm 91:1).

Affirmations

- Be still, my soul, and be silent.
- I love the silence with God.
- God meets me in silence.
- I love the presence of God in my silence.
- I make it a priority to set time aside for silence with God.
- Silence is teaching me the first language of God.

BREATHE

The LORD God formed man of the dust of the ground,
and breathed into his nostrils the breath of life;
and man became a living soul.

GENESIS 2:7 KJV

The spirit of God hath made me, and the breath of the
Almighty hath given me life.

JOB 33:4 KJV

When he had said this, he breathed on them,
and saith unto them, Receive ye the Holy Ghost.

JOHN 20:22 KJV

Meditate

Try this exercise: Sitting still with your eyes gently closed,
inhale very slowly while silently whispering the name Jesus.
As you slowly exhale your breath, silently whisper the name
Jesus again. Keep your breath moving very slowly and
evenly, no rushing or gasping, just keep your breath flowing
smoothly until you sense the name of Jesus becoming a part
of your breath.

You have to admit we take breathing for granted
and rarely tell ourselves, *Hey, I'm breathing*, unless there's a
problem with our breathing. "Let everything that breathes
praise the LORD" (Psalm 150:6 NRSVUE). That's you. You
have breath, and with your breath, you constantly praise
the Lord.

The Hebrew word for "breath," *ruach*, is the same word for "spirit" or "wind." *Ruach* is the breath of God breathing into your lungs right now. You and I exist because God breathed his breath into Adam, the first human. You have God's breath in you too. When you breathe in the name Jesus, he breathes your breath. Do it now: breathe in Jesus...breathe out Jesus...

Continue to do the breathing exercise above. Allow yourself to rest in the awareness of the breath of God in you and through you. During the day, be aware of his breath bringing life to all created beings. The world is suffocating itself, but God's children live in the goodness of his love with every breath.[1]

Affirmations

- I breathe in the breath of God, and he breathes his breath in me.
- I focus on the breath God has given me by taking nice, deep, slow breaths and silently whispering the name Jesus.
- Focusing on the breath of God in me gives me supernatural peace.
- With all my breath, I will praise the Lord.
- Breath is holy, and I honor the *ruach* of God breathing life and power into my lungs and my body.

---

1 To learn more about breath practice, visit QuietPrayer.org.

MAKING CHOICES

"You did not choose Me, but I chose you and appointed
you that you should go and bear fruit, and that your fruit
should remain, that whatever you ask the Father in My
name He may give you."

JOHN 15:16

Meditate

Choice is what controls everything we do, say, think, and
believe. The Hebrew Bible uses the words *choose* and
choice and their variants 246 times. *Choose* and *choice*
appear fifty-nine times in the King James Version of the
New Testament. When your choices bless the Lord, you'll
experience your days far more fully because you'll take
charge of the choices you make. David made this command
of his soul in Psalm 34:1: "I will bless the LORD at all times;
His praise shall continually be in my mouth." To command
your soul to bless the Lord is a choice.

Behind everything you do is a choice, from brushing
your teeth to showing up at your in-laws' anniversary
party, from buying a new car to scratching your nose. You
stand up, sit down, lie down, look in the mirror, eat an egg,
dance—all choices. To pray or not to pray, to love God or
not to love God are choices. You take command over your
life by taking command over your choices.

Some choices you make determine your entire life.
Joshua, being fed up with people who were following false
gods, commanded them to "choose for yourselves this day

whom you will serve" (Joshua 24:15). When Joshua said "choose," he was talking about a life choice.

Look at the choices you make. In the morning when you rise, give the Lord the many choices you'll make during the day. He will send his Holy Spirit to guide, nudge, and lovingly steer you as you make life-fulfilling choices. You can't live without making choices. By being aware of this fact, you will be far more equipped to follow the path God has set before you.

Take extra time now with the affirmations. You choose whether to be upset during the day or to remain calm. You choose whether to practice stillness or go through the day feeling the sting of its turmoil. You have the privilege of choosing God because he already chose you (John 15:16). He chose you before the very foundation of the world (Ephesians 1:4).

Affirmations

- I choose right now—this minute—whom I will serve (Joshua 24:14–15).
- I love and serve God only.
- I make it a priority to think and pray about my choices.
- I'm responsible for the choices I make in my life.
- I do not blame situations, events, or people for my poor choices.
- I ask the Holy Spirit every day to guide, nudge, and steer me in the path God has set before me.

COMPASSION AND MERCY

He is good to everyone, and his compassion
is intertwined with everything he does.
PSALM 145:9 TLB

His compassion never ends. It is only the Lord's mercies
that have kept us from complete destruction.
LAMENTATIONS 3:22 TLB

Meditate

When Jesus told us to cast our cares on him, he took
humanity on his shoulders. His compassion and mercy
shape, maintain, and build our faith as Christians.

In the parable of the unmerciful servant (Matthew
18:21–35), the master shows mercy and great kindness to
the man who owes him a lot of money by forgiving the debt
entirely. It was an act of mercy.

There is a difference between compassion and mercy.
Mercy is forgiving someone when it's within one's power to
punish or harm them. Mercy isn't always compassionate.
A person can show mercy without feeling compassion.
Mercy by itself forgives and does good but not necessarily
with compassion. A judge can show mercy by pronouncing
a lenient sentence on a defendant, but compassion isn't
necessarily an influencing factor in the case. Similarly, we
can feel compassion but not show mercy. Compassion
means sympathetic pity and concern for the sufferings or
misfortunes of others. We can show pity or concern for

someone but not necessarily act on it. We can feel sorry for someone, but we don't necessarily act on the feeling. It is only a feeling. God, however, always acts with both mercy and compassion on our behalf.

When Jesus tells us to be merciful as our Father is merciful, he is not just telling us what to do but also telling us how to do it. Jesus tells us to forgive our enemies, which is mercy, and he says to love our enemies, which is compassion. In our Christian tradition, the virtue of solidarity bridges both compassion and mercy. Compassion and mercy meet one another in us when we feel compassion toward others and do something about it. Micah 6:8 explains our calling: "He has shown you, O man, what is good; and what does the LORD require of you but to do justly, to love mercy, and to walk humbly with your God?" God's mercy and compassion are forever.

Affirmations

- I have compassion living in me. I only have to reach into my soul to find God's compassion there.
- My compassion brings out God's mercy in me.
- God has shown me the way to please him, and I will walk with both mercy and compassion.
- I love showing mercy and acting on my compassion.
- I am not afraid of what mercy might cost me, nor am I afraid to show compassion.
- I show mercy and compassion even when I don't think the other person deserves it.

GOD'S BEST FOR ME

"The LORD will guide you continually, and satisfy your soul
in drought, and strengthen your bones; you shall be like a
watered garden, and like a spring of water, whose waters do
not fail."

ISAIAH 58:11

"I know the plans I have for you, declares the LORD, plans
for welfare and not for evil, to give you a future and a hope."

JEREMIAH 29:11 ESV

We know that for those who love God
all things work together for good,
for those who are called according to his purpose.

ROMANS 8:28 ESV

Meditate

Aren't success, prosperity, love, and a good family God's
best for me? The answers seep into my spirit slowly as
I spend more time alone with God. When we pray for
something or someone, we ask God to do what we believe
is right according to Scripture, and of course that's good.
But there's more.

If I am one with God and he is one with me, my
entire existence belongs to him. I make affirmations not
because of what I want but because of who he is—and who
we are together. I invited Jesus into my life when I said yes
and surrendered myself completely to him. Because I am
his child, he lives in me by his Holy Spirit, and I am now

conscious of living in his perfect love. Each passing year brings new vistas of his love to discover, treasure, and share.

Painful and tragic events don't feel like God's best for me. A common question people ask God is *why*. We'll never come up with a satisfying answer to why bad things happen to good people except to know God is a giver of good, not bad (Jeremiah 29:11). I move from pain to empowerment and know my circumstances are God's best for me. I miss out on God's best when my faith sinks and I don't go to his Word for wisdom and strength.

Pray to the Lord like David did: "Surely your goodness and love will follow me all the days of my life" (Psalm 23:6 NIV). When you focus on God's power working in you in all situations and circumstances, your faith will not falter but grow stronger. Affirm and speak God's Word to your soul several times during the day.

Affirmations

- What I think is the best for me may not be what God thinks is the best for me.
- The Lord guides me and satisfies my soul in drought and strengthens my bones (Isaiah 58:11).
- Goodness and love follow me all the days of my life.
- I don't settle for less than God's best for me.
- I do not pursue shallow promises of happiness and success.
- I am strong.
- I am whole.

THE POWER OF LOVE

Hope does not disappoint, because the love of God
has been poured out in our hearts by the Holy Spirit
who was given to us.
ROMANS 5:5

"The life which I now live in the flesh I live by faith in the
Son of God, who loved me and gave Himself for me."
GALATIANS 2:20

Jesus said to him, "'You shall love the LORD your God with
all your heart, with all your soul, and with all your mind.'"
MATTHEW 22:37

Meditate

Give yourself permission to accept that you are loved. Love
is God himself. Love is the transforming factor giving you
life. Deep inside you is your greatest treasure, which is God,
and God is love. Love finds love and multiplies itself in the
loved one. God is love, and God cannot resist himself.

Take a minute to breathe in the word *love*. Then
gently close your eyes, let your body relax, and sit quietly
with Jesus without saying a word. It doesn't have to be for
long; simply breathe deeply, speak the word *love*, and sit
with Jesus. If you do this regularly during your daily walk,
it won't be long before you find a noticeable change taking
place in your attitudes and behavior. Breathing in the
presence of God is a miraculous undertaking of the Holy

Spirit, and there's no way to fake it. This practice becomes more personal as you continue taking these love breaks.

You learn about love by living for God. He wants you to know him deeply, intimately, and personally. He wants you to think like him. You learn about love by learning about God. Nothing should stop you because you already have the mind of Christ (1 Corinthians 2:16). Sometimes it's through tragedy and sorrow that you discover how loved you truly are. God's love breaks through pain to see beyond it. It's this life-transforming realization of God's intense and personal love for you that keeps expanding in you.

God himself has revealed the secrets of loving and being loved in Scripture. Only he and his love define love. The power of love is to know God. Knowing him, we learn to see ourselves through the eyes of love. There are no other eyes with which to see the world as it truly is. First Corinthians 13:12 in *The Message* affirms our lack of love's illumination this way: "We don't yet see things clearly. We're squinting in a fog, peering through a mist." Only love sees through the mist.

Affirmations

- The Lord's love continuously draws me to him.
- I do not confuse God's love with human love.
- God's love is pouring into my heart right now.
- The love of God is the very foundation of the world's existence, whether the world knows it or not.
- I dedicate my life to knowing and loving God.

WHEN MY SOUL BLESSES GOD

Bless the LORD, O my soul; and all that is within me, bless His holy name! Bless the LORD, O my soul, and forget not all His benefits: who forgives all your iniquities, who heals all your diseases, who redeems your life from destruction, who crowns you with lovingkindness and tender mercies, who satisfies your mouth with good things, so that your youth is renewed like the eagle's.

PSALM 103:1–5

Meditate

In Psalm 103, David ordered his soul to bless the Lord, which translates to mean he ordered his soul to gratefully praise God. This wasn't just a one-time or occasional activity for David. The human soul craves to bless the Lord. David itemized five of God's benefits and told us not to forget them. One, God forgives our sins. Two, he heals all our diseases. Three, he rescues our lives from the pit of hell. Four, he crowns us lavishly with his loving-kindness and tender mercies by satisfying our years with good things. And five, he restores our youth.

A lifestyle of praise from the depths of our souls opens the door to living in these benefits as a matter of course. Praise changes us from inside.

We can praise and honor God in a worship service or in our personal prayer time, but it's different when we command our souls to bless the Lord with praise at all times. With praise, our souls, our intellects, our emotions, and our wills pause to drop the fuss, quiet down, and focus on the reality of the greatness of God. We put an end to our egocentric reactions to life's events, and we stop the clutter that dominates our thinking. We order our souls to gratefully praise God as a lifestyle every day and ideally all day. We make an effort and create change. David demanded his soul to praise the Lord, and that's what it takes to get our souls in sync with God, who is in us as we are in him.

Our souls can be unruly with mental clutter, uncontrolled feelings, and impaired decision-making. Our souls can be so influenced by the world that we confuse darkness with light. Nobody else can command your soul to do anything. Your soul is yours to command, control, and keep holy. You and I possess the massive inner resolve to bless the Lord with our human souls. His benefits aren't far away in the distance. His Word is forever (Isaiah 40:8). Take charge of your soul with your mind, emotions, and will and command every aspect of it to bless the Lord today and every day.

Affirmations

- I tell my soul to be a blessing to God.
- I thank God for his benefits, and I won't forget them.

FOCUS

Seek those things which are above, where Christ is, sitting at the right hand of God. Set your mind on things above, not on things on the earth.

<small>Colossians 3:1-2</small>

Because he has focused his love on me, I will deliver him. I will protect him because he knows my name.

<small>Psalm 91:14 ISV</small>

My son, stay focused; listen to the wisdom I have gained; give attention to what I have learned about life so you may be able to make sensible judgments and speak with knowledge.

<small>Proverbs 5:1-2 VOICE</small>

Meditate

The idea of focus is similar to the word *seek*, as in "seek first the kingdom of God" (Matthew 6:33). God wants us to focus on obtaining what we seek. Focus is something we learn through practice. That's why we spend time speaking the affirmations in this book. With each affirmation, we are focusing on God's truth. This is good exercise for our brains as well as our souls and spirits. We build new neural pathways of truth to counteract the old, negative neural pathways in our brains. We have developed bad habits in our thinking that can be damaging in many ways because we're products of the way we think. Our behavior is in direct response to what we tell ourselves. The negative habits can fade, and new habits are formed. Negative neural pathways are like ruts in the brain that we fall into easily when faced with life's challenges.

Paul told the Hebrews to keep their focus on Jesus (Hebrews 3:1). Isaiah wrote that God will keep our minds in perfect peace when we stay focused on him (Isaiah 26:3).

We can learn to focus through daily practice. By setting moments aside to focus on God and his Word, you will be building new habits of focus and new neural pathways in the brain. Scientific research has shown that it only takes twenty-one days to form a new habit. Withdraw each day to a quiet place to be alone with God. Sit with your eyes gently closed. Allow yourself to breathe slowly and evenly, and for now, focus on just one aspect of the Lord you love. Take your time. Turn your attention to his loving-kindness. Breathe in his presence, and he will reveal himself to you. Focus on a portion of Scripture, such as Colossians 2:10, and say, *I am complete in Christ.* Continue to silently repeat the words as you sit quietly in the presence of God. Try to remain quietly focused for two to ten minutes.

Affirmations

- I'm building new neural pathways in my brain by taking time to focus on God and not myself.
- I focus on beautiful things and not negative things that take me away from the truth and love of God.
- I practice focusing on God to expand my prayer life.
- I pray with more confidence as I learn to focus.

VISUALIZATION

Now faith is being sure of what we hope for,
being convinced of what we do not see.
HEBREWS 11:1 NET

"Assuredly, I say to you, if you have faith as a mustard seed,
you will say to this mountain, 'Move from here to there,'
and it will move; and nothing will be impossible for you."
MATTHEW 17:20

Meditate

We all have different gifts and talents. How far we go with those gifts can depend on how hard we work. Take swimmer Michael Phelps, for example. Rather than just going from good to great, he shattered Olympic records when he competed from 2000 to 2016. He has won the most Olympic medals in all Olympic history to this very day with twenty-three gold medals, three silver, and two bronze.

Phelps's former coach, Bob Bowman, revealed that one secret to Phelps's stunning success was his mental readiness. For two hours a day, Phelps would mentally go over all potential scenarios of the race and all sensory elements: the feel and sound of the water, the smell of the air, the noise of the crowds in the stands, the sensation of the air in his lungs.[2]

---

2 Carmine Gallo, "3 Daily Habits of Peak Performers, according to Michael Phelps' Coach," *Forbes* (website), May 24, 2016, https://www.forbes.com/sites/carminegallo/2016/05/24/3-daily-habits-of-peak-performers-according-to-michael-phelps-coach/?sh=6ff833c1102c.

How does visualization fit into our Christian lives? Maintain a strong belief in who you are as a child of God and see yourself as strong and brave, as an overcomer. Remember that everything you can think of, you can attain through the Holy Spirit and maintain through Christ. Go to those areas of challenge and visualize just how you'll handle them. This takes time. Remember Michael Phelps spent two hours every day visualizing a race before getting in the water. What about the time we spend every day with God?

You are a child of God with a strong belief in who you are and your purpose here on earth. When you believe who you are and who you want to be tomorrow, *visualize* it. You may not have an eighty-inch wingspan like Michael Phelps, but you have faith to move mountains and a great future in Christ awaiting you. The wonderful result of visualization is that you literally reprogram your brain to focus on the truth as revealed in God's Word. Live it.

Affirmations

- I see myself as an overcomer.
- I see myself handling the challenge before me with integrity and faith that moves mountains.
- I see myself going within for the love I don't feel now.
- I see myself conquering fear, depression, and envy that have plagued me for so long.
- I tell myself the truth, and I am transformed by the love of Christ.

DECLUTTERING MY MIND

Finally, brethren, whatever things are true, whatever things are noble, whatever things are just, whatever things are pure, whatever things are lovely, whatever things are of good report, if there is any virtue and if there is anything praiseworthy—meditate on these things.

Philippians 4:8

Meditate

This verse from Philippians is one of the most important verses in the New Testament about paying attention to the power of our thought lives. Only when we work at decluttering our minds are we able to focus. The power of focus directly affects the clutter we've allowed to fill our minds. The artist Pablo Picasso is credited with saying, "Art is the elimination of the unnecessary." Our minds need an elimination of the unnecessary.

When decluttering our minds, we aren't removing all thinking; we're managing our thinking. Paul's letter to the Philippians is genius kingdom advice, and modern-day Christian counselors and leaders would do well to seriously, and with regularity, study and practice Paul's brilliant, detailed strategy for decluttering the mind. This could change the entire spiritual climate of God's church. Ephesians 5:27 reads, "That He [Jesus] might present her [the church] to Himself a glorious church, not *having spot or wrinkle or any such thing, but that she should be holy and without blemish*" (emphasis added). Spots and blemishes begin in the mind. It's our thoughts that soil our hearts and soil relationships and even our walk with the Lord.

Sitting silently in the presence of God helps quiet you down as unruly thoughts whizz through your head. But as you bring your focus to God in the silence, take some nice deep breaths and relax your body. Gently brush aside the unwanted thoughts with a Scripture verse. Try to remain quietly focused for two to ten minutes. It only takes a minute with the Lord, and it's a lifetime journey.

As you read Philippians 4:8, name each of the areas of focus Paul gave: true, noble, just, pure, lovely, of good report, virtuous, and worthiness of praise. Do this very slowly over a period of days. Take time to focus on one thing a day. Make some notes as you contemplate the words. You're building new positive neural pathways in your brain as you focus on that which is beautiful. Romans 12:2 says the only way we're transformed is by the renewing of our minds.

Affirmations

- In the name of Jesus, I am becoming more aware of the way I think. I can learn to focus and quiet the clutter in my mind (2 Corinthians 10:5).
- I focus on one word in Philippians 4:8 per day.
- I will be transformed by the renewing of my mind.
- I build new neural pathways in my brain as I learn to declutter my mind daily with new Jesus-centered habits of concentration and focus.

LIVING RIGHT NOW

"Do not be anxious about tomorrow, for tomorrow will be anxious for itself. Sufficient for the day is its own trouble."
MATTHEW 6:34 ESV

Whatever you do, in word or deed, do everything in the name of the Lord Jesus, giving thanks to God the Father through him.
COLOSSIANS 3:17 ESV

Meditate

"Give us this day," we pray in the Lord's Prayer. This is a "right now" prayer. We're asking the Lord to give to us right now. We sing Psalm 118:24 with David, "This is the day the LORD has made," focusing on right now, today, not tomorrow or next week or yesterday. God has given us "this day."

In Paul's letter to the Christians at Corinth, he writes, "Whether you eat or drink, or whatever you do, do all to the glory of God" (1 Corinthians 10:31 ESV). This is a good example of living right now because when we eat, we're doing it right now. Eating and drinking to the glory of God means we're paying attention to the process of chewing, swallowing, sipping, tasting, burping, gulping—everything eating and drinking include.

When you make a conscious decision to be aware of right now, you'll learn to love and respect time. Bring your attention back to the present moment. The air, the smells, the things around you, outside, inside, the sounds, the movements of your body. Turn your attention to the task or activity your hands are touching. What does it feel like in your hands? What colors are you seeing? Can you see God? What do the words "in everything give thanks" (1 Thessalonians 5:18) mean to you?

Develop this skill of paying attention to the present moment and watch how your attention to detail improves. Your power of focus improves. Your understanding, patience, and ability to laugh and enjoy yourself and others improve.

Fulfill Colossians 3:17 by being alive and conscious of the moment. "Whatever you do in word or deed, do all in the name of the Lord Jesus."

Affirmations

- I am alive right now.
- I don't live in the future when things will get better.
- I don't live in the past when things were better.
- I don't live in the past when things were worse.
- I control my daydreaming and mind wandering.
- The expression "I live for today" is not specific enough. I live for each moment of each day.
- My mind is clear and sharp.
- I make a conscious choice to be aware of what my moments hold for me and for God.

I HAVE DIVINE PURPOSE

I know the thoughts that I think toward you,
says the LORD, thoughts of peace and not of evil.
JEREMIAH 29:11

Thus Noah did; according to all that God commanded him,
so he did.
GENESIS 6:22

Meditate

No purpose of God is too difficult or outrageous. Consider
Noah. If ever there was a character in the Bible with a
difficult and outrageous purpose, it was Noah. His entire
life was focused on one thing: building an impossible
structure called an ark for an impossible reason. It took
him almost seventy-five years of labor to do it, much of
the project completed under the derision of his neighbors.
God worked with him all the way, encouraging, directing,
instructing, explaining what he wanted and how to do it,
and Noah did his job without a hitch.

I might add that Noah was five hundred years old
when his sons were born, so are we ever too old or too
young to fulfill an outrageous thing for God? No.

You have a purpose, too, and it's no less important
than that of Noah. What God looks at is your obedience.
"Obedience is far better than sacrifice. He is much more
interested in your listening to him than in your [other]
offering" (1 Samuel 15:22 TLB).

God likes working with you as you fulfill your divine purpose just like Noah. How do I know this? Because God has said it. Romans 2:11 says, "There is no partiality with God." We are all God's favorite. Be comfortable and at peace with the importance of your purpose in God. Begin now to affirm your confidence in your purpose and calling. Read the following affirmations aloud and really listen.

Affirmations

- God thinks about me and doesn't fill me with futile ambitions.
- I am careful not to confuse my purpose in life with the influences of popular culture.
- No one has a purpose more important than mine, and my purpose is no more important than anyone else's.
- I love my calling and purpose in the Lord.
- Even when I feel like I have no purpose, I have a purpose.
- I have full confidence in the Lord's plan for my life.
- There is no doubt or confusion in me about my purpose in life.
- Every day I invite God into the welcoming home of my heart.

NO MORE COMPLAINING

Do all things without grumbling.
PHILIPPIANS 2:14 ESV

Meditate

Try to curb your complaining with sheer willpower, and what happens? More complaining. It's like asking a bicycle to do the work of a truck. Any change we need to make in our lives requires the work of the Holy Spirit, not our willpower. Have you ever noticed how we complain to God and call it prayer? To recognize and put an end to complaining starts with repenting. God gave us nine simple words to radically yank us from the swamp of complaining: "Resist the devil, and he will flee from you" (James 4:7 NIV). Complaining is an enemy of God, who blesses us beyond what we ask for.

My mother was an exceptional woman. She would thank God for the smallest thing—a new dish towel, lipstick, the color blue. No matter how tough things got, she didn't complain. It was my mother who taught me what it means to love life.

We can't wholly love life, or anything else for that matter, if we maintain the joy-draining habit of complaining. I sometimes give my counseling clients a homework assignment to say thank you five times a day. It can be a life changer. The Spirit of God lives in gratitude. Not all my clients could say thank you five times a day right away. But it wasn't long before they were saying the words *thank you* twenty times and more a day. We honor God with a thankful heart.

Complaining closes and locks the door to the experience of joy in your life. When Job stopped focusing on his miserable situation in Job 13:15, he made the affirmation that has inspired generations of believers: "Though He slay me, yet will I trust Him." He had lost everything he owned; he lost his children, livestock, workers, and he was covered in oozing boils. In the presence of love, Job saw his complaints as shallow. It was God's presence that humbled him, and it's God's presence that humbles you and me. I can almost hear God asking us, as he did Job, "Where were you when I laid the earth's foundation?" (38:4 NIV). Complaining is an insult to God, who has given us his eyes and ears of wisdom and compassion to behold the world.

Affirmations

- I am content in Christ, and I don't complain.
- I choose not to be around people who complain.
- I say the words *thank you* at least five times a day.
- I thank Jesus for showing me how to open my eyes to what is good.
- I do not complain so I can love the life God has given me.
- I do not complain to God and call it prayer.
- Though God slay me, I will trust him.
- I have absolutely nothing to complain about.

I'M RIGHTEOUS

I pray this…that you can decide what is best, and thus be sincere and blameless for the day of Christ, filled with the fruit of righteousness that comes through Jesus Christ to the glory and praise of God.

PHILIPPIANS 1:9–11 NET

Meditate

The word *righteous* in the Bible often appears with the words *sanctification* and *redemption*. What is meant by these words, and what's the difference between righteousness and sanctification?

The spiritual meaning of *righteousness* is to be right in the eyes of God, including our character, conscience, attitudes, conduct, speech, actions, and obedience. Whew. Is it even possible? The good news is that Christians who give their lives to Jesus become righteous in the eyes of God because it's the righteousness of Jesus that we possess. Each of the attributes of righteousness illustrates the person of Christ Jesus. There are 558 references to the righteous in the Bible, and there are 9 references to the righteousness of Christ in the New Testament. Jesus assigns his right standing with God to us, so when God looks at you and me, he sees his Son in us and not what we were before we came to him.

In Matthew 6:33, Jesus told us to "seek first the kingdom of God and His righteousness." We are to pursue and run toward the kingdom of God, which is God himself.

As children of God, we seek and find the kingdom of God in the presence of God. Jesus said in Matthew 7:7 to "seek, and you will find." The word *seek* encompasses the word *find*. In faith it's one act.

Affirmations

- I welcome Jesus and his righteousness in my heart and life.
- I live my life on God's terms.
- I seek the kingdom of God in Christ, and in seeking him, I find him.
- I'm righteous in the sight of God, who sees his Son in me.
- I am forgiven of my sins and of missing the mark with the Lord, and I live in right standing with God.

FAITH

Jesus said to them, "Because of your unbelief; for assuredly, I say to you, if you have faith as a mustard seed, you will say to this mountain, 'Move from here to there,' and it will move; and nothing will be impossible for you."

MATTHEW 17:20

Without faith it is impossible to please Him, for he who comes to God must believe that He is, and that He is a rewarder of those who diligently seek Him.

HEBREWS 11:6

Meditate

A true story of faith that has stayed with me for years is about a Yugoslav family during the dictatorship of Tito and the Second World War.[3] The mother was taken from her children and forced to fight with Tito's resistance movement against the Germans. They were a little group of untrained civilians with sticks instead of rifles. One day, they sat exhausted in a clearing, and Jozeca, the mother, began praising the Lord, which she was always doing, much to the fury of her companions. She began to tell the man beside her about Jesus and that just to know him was enough for her to praise him all day long. She told the man God loved him too. He, a dialectical materialist and atheist to the bone, growled back at her that he would believe God loved him when polenta rained down from the sky. Jozeca put her

---

3 For more information on this story, see my book *Of Whom the World Was Not Worthy*.

trust in God and prayed. Not many days later, American planes flew overhead, dropping down care packages, and inside them were bags of polenta.

For me, Jozeca is the perfect example of a woman with total faith in the love of God with no loopholes, not the tiniest doubt, no hesitations, no backsteps, and absolutely no fear.

Faith for the child of God is like Jozeca's deep spiritual assurance in the reality of God and his love. True faith is complete trust and confidence in the God of all creation and his Son, Jesus. It's our foundation, the substance of every breath we take, the basis of our purpose as human beings. Faith is both substance and evidence of things hoped for and unseen (Hebrews 11:1). Invisible to the natural eye, faith is the substance that produces substance. Faith is transforming power. Keep growing in it.

Affirmations

- God's promises to me are forever, and therefore, I trust him forever (2 Peter 3:9).
- I have faith to move mountains.
- The Holy Spirit lives in me, and God cannot deny himself (2 Timothy 2:13).
- My faith in God is continuously growing (Romans 1:17).
- I live by faith, not by sight (2 Corinthians 5:7).
- I have faith for the impossible.

HIS CROSS, MY CROSS

He said to them all, "If anyone wants to become my follower, he must deny himself, take up his cross daily, and follow me."

LUKE 9:23 NET

Meditate

"Take up your cross and follow me" was a startling thing to hear in Jesus' day considering what the cross represented at the time. In his day, the cross was an instrument of torture that inspired terror. When Jesus spoke of the cross, he was preparing his disciples and us for future suffering. He concluded with three words, "and follow me," three assuring, empowering words. He was telling them, "Do as I do. See how I handle suffering. Be brave with unshakable faith."

Jesus knew the disciples would suffer persecution and death for his sake. He was encouraging them to be strong, like him, and to follow his example.

Today we carry a cross too. Our crosses come in many different forms, and we'll carry many in our lifetimes. Your cross can be your heaviest burden, the one that may be so painful that it could kill you. Always your cross has to do with the impact of faith in you. Your natural strength, good intentions, positive thinking, resolution making, and so-called letting go can't possibly conquer spiritual powers. The crosses the disciples carried required enormous spiritual power along with their love for the Lord.

Galatians 2:20 explains what our cross is: "I have been crucified with Christ, and it is no longer I who live, but Christ lives in me. So the life I now live in the body, I live because of the faithfulness of the Son of God, who loved me and gave himself for me" (NET).

An example of someone who took up his cross is Father Junípero Serra, founder of over twenty missions in California. At the end of his life, he was in terrible pain and dying from ulcerations on his chest. When the surgeon arrived at the mission, he found the missionary not lying miserably in the infirmary but at work sewing garments for the children.[4] He took up his cross and followed (imitated, became like) Jesus.

Let's look at our own lives for the integrity we've shown carrying our crosses. Dying physically is not that hard to do. We're all going to do it one day. It's the Holy Spirit's life of spiritual integrity in us, our acceptance, and the dynamic eternal force of our faith that sweeps us into the glorious purpose of our cross and his cross.

Affirmations

- I am not afraid of suffering.
- I carry my crosses with integrity.
- I do not feel sorry for myself.
- I do not demand my life to be free of hardship or suffering.
- I stand fast in faith. I'm brave, and I'm strong (1 Corinthians 16:13).
- I reject the power of pain over my peace of mind.

---

4 Agnes Repplier, *Junipero Serra: Pioneer Colonist of California* (New York: Doubleday, 1933), 252.

CONSTANTLY GROWING FAITH

It is good…to declare Your lovingkindness in the morning,
and Your faithfulness every night.
PSALM 92:1–2

Faith is the substance of things hoped for,
the evidence of things not seen.
HEBREWS 11:1

The prayer of faith will save the sick, and the Lord will raise
him up. And if he has committed sins, he will be forgiven.
JAMES 5:15

Meditate

The universe as God created it is always in motion, and it's
the same with our faith in God as his children. Faith is a
living substance (Hebrews 11:1), alive and in motion. True
faith is never inert because it's alive. It's the lack of faith
that renders itself lifeless and going nowhere. The universe
we live in is continuously in motion through gravitation
and electromagnetic forces. It's interesting to note that if
there were no magnetic forces, the universe would have
no movement. There is a powerful spiritual force at work
in you, growing your faith and keeping it alive. Science
still can't fully explain the forces keeping the universe in
motion, and our faith in motion is an even greater mystery.

Read Hebrews 11 and see yourself in each of the heroes
of faith. You're there. Power keeps growing in the storehouse
of your faith. You're a universe in the kingdom of God.

Affirmations

- I am a person of enormous faith.
- My faith constantly grows.
- My faith keeps developing and expanding as I pray and read God's Word.
- My faith is never at a standstill.
- My faith is never dead.
- My faith in God makes me a loving person.
- The deeper my faith in God is, the more loving I am.
- I'm a very loving person.
- I will always be a loving person because my faith in God keeps on growing and growing.
- First Corinthians 15:58 says to "be steadfast, immovable, always abounding in the work of the Lord," and that's what I am. I'm steadfast, and my faith is on the move.

20

TURNING BAD TO GOOD

"As for you, you meant evil against me, but God meant it
for good in order to bring about this present result."
GENESIS 50:20 NASB

Do not be overcome by evil,
but overcome evil with good.
ROMANS 12:21

Meditate

What are the feelings that we experience when bad
things happen? Good things that happen aren't usually
as emotional as when bad things happen. Also, the good
feelings don't last as long as the bad feelings. For example,
you may have received an unexpected check in the mail and
felt very happy and excited, and a year later, chances are you
won't even remember it. But if you lost your wallet, you'd
remember it for years.

Here is one way to get from bad to good, beginning
with your emotions. Take anger, for instance. Say you're
wrongly accused, and you're outraged. The key is to
separate your negative emotion, anger, from being wrongly
accused. You don't realize it right away, but your anger is
actually an opportunity. By turning your attention to your
feeling, not the situation, you have the opportunity to turn
bad (anger) to good (acceptance).

With acceptance you remove anger's power over
you, making it possible to hear from God and handle the

situation free of anger's grip. A little time goes by, and you may have empathy toward the person or people who made the false accusation. God breathes on your inner wisdom, and you turn a potentially long-lasting, combative situation into a friendly one.

In 1995 Jean-Dominique Bauby was the successful editor-in-chief of the French fashion magazine *Elle*. Married with two young children, he was suddenly stricken with a rare condition called locked-in syndrome, for which there is no cure. He was entirely paralyzed except for one eye, which he could blink. In this condition, unable to move or talk, he dictated a beautiful book entitled *The Diving Bell and the Butterfly* by blinking each letter with one eye.[5] Starting with acceptance, he used the only moving part of his body to write his memoir.

Affirmations

- I can turn a bad feeling and situation into something creative and beautiful.
- When bad things happen, I immediately calm down to hear from God.
- I bring wisdom to bad situations by turning my negative emotional reactions into opportunities for change.
- God opens opportunities to create good even out of the worst situations.

---

5   Janine Di Giovanni, "The Real Love Story Behind *The Diving Bell and the Butterfly*," *Guardian*, November 29, 2008, https://www.theguardian.com/lifeandstyle/2008/nov/30/diving-bell-butterfly-florence-bensadoun.

21

GUILT AND SHAME

There is therefore now no condemnation to those who are
in Christ Jesus, who do not walk according to the flesh,
but according to the Spirit.

ROMANS 8:1

"Their sins and their lawless deeds
I will remember no more."

HEBREWS 10:17

If the Son makes you free,
you shall be free indeed.

JOHN 8:36

Meditate

When you were a child, did adults ever give you the
squinted eye with the reprimand "Shame on you"? Now
as grown-ups, we can live out those words as we gather up
more things to be ashamed of. Shame is something we all
feel at some time or another. Guilt is something we also
feel, but shame and guilt are not the same.

Shame screams about what a terrible person you are.
Guilt screams that something you did was wrong. Guilt for
having done something bad can quickly lead to negative
thoughts about who you are as a person, which is shame.
Guilt usually leads to remorse that accepts responsibility
for what happened and fosters the redemptive desire to be
forgiven. It calls for action and seeks solutions. Because
shame is rooted in how you see yourself, it's easier to let it

ferment inside. A person who feels shame without remorse can remain trapped in self-judgment and feelings of inferiority.

It's important to recognize the feelings of shame and guilt and then take action to be free of them. The Lord Jesus gave his life for our freedom from guilt and shame. First, before doing anything else, ask for forgiveness. You can't do a thing about guilt without asking for forgiveness. Pour out your heart to God. Tell him everything. He has taken all our guilt on himself: "I, I am he who blots out your transgressions for my own sake, and I will not remember your sins" (Isaiah 43:25 ESV). The Holy Spirit will guide you in making amends and changes in your life. Forgiveness transforms us.

Find a quiet place where you can open your heart to Jesus. (Shame will try to convince you to avoid God.) Look inside yourself for shame that you may have been carrying for years. When you drop all shame into the lap of Jesus, you not only free yourself, but you honor and glorify him.

Affirmations

- I ask forgiveness from God and release myself from the pain of guilt.
- I release, in the name of Jesus, all feelings of shame.
- Jesus suffered terrible shame for my sake, and I will not hold on to shame when his love and compassion have set me free.
- I now live a new life free of guilt and shame for the glory of God.

22

NEVER ALONE

He Himself has said,
"I will never leave you nor forsake you."
HEBREWS 13:5

Meditate

Loneliness is feeling separate or separated from other people. A woman I was seeing in my counseling practice told me she felt totally alone and that she felt being alone was a curse and that she would die alone. She didn't feel lonely around her pets (three cats and a dog), but she felt completely alienated from human relationships. After some time, she began to see that she believed approval was something she had to earn.

We learn feelings the same way we learn ideas. When punished for bad behavior rather than appropriately disciplined, some children learn that they're the ones who are bad, not the behavior. "Bad girl!" and "Bad boy!" are popular expressions adults use every day. As we become adults, these false ideas about ourselves can still float around in our minds like little sinking boats, dragging us down without our realizing what's happening. *I'm only good if I act good*, thinks the child who, as an adult, goes on to think like a child, believing they have to earn love and approval.

Jesus died on the cross for our sins, and now we have the freedom to know and live in truth. My client had taught herself to believe that (1) she wasn't good enough, (2) she would not meet others' expectations, (3) she had nothing to offer anyone, and (4) others would always reject her. Slowly she began to see how her deeply embedded ideas had nothing to do with the truth. She decided to set herself free from the past and realized that she was acceptable and likable even if imperfect.

It's our imperfections we dread, although God never turns his head from us because of our imperfections. Accepting our imperfections sets us on our way to wholeness.

Sometimes we think we aren't good enough for the world or the opposite—that the world isn't good enough for us. Both false beliefs are alienating. All of us feel alone at times, so it's crucial to always be aware of your self-talk. Take notes. Make a list. For every lie you write down, respond with the truth. If you write down, "People won't like me," write next to it, "I am likable."

Affirmations

- I am loved and appreciated.
- Approval is not something I have to earn.
- I see very clearly that the Lord Jesus is right here with me and within me. I am part of his family.
- I will not push people away with my false feelings of inferiority.
- I am lovable and fun to be with.
- I renounce every lie that I learned as a child about not being good enough.

23

LONELINESS

God sets the solitary in families.
PSALM 68:6

God makes a home for the lonely;
He leads the prisoners into prosperity,
only the stubborn and rebellious dwell in a parched land.
PSALM 68:6 AMP

I have become like a lonely bird on a housetop.
PSALM 102:7 AMP

Meditate

Throughout Christian history, we can see that many men
and women lived solitary lives alone with God because
they chose him above earthly relationships and comforts
of the world. They lived lives of asceticism, abstinence, and
discipline to give themselves solely to God. They focused
on his Word and prayer. In the research I've conducted on
these venerated men and women of God from Origen to
Thomas Merton, I have yet to find one who complained of
being lonely.

The word *lonely* doesn't appear in the New
Testament and only appears in the Old Testament when
referring to loss. Biblically, loneliness differs from feelings
of being alone. *Alone* means to feel separate, apart from
others. *Loneliness* refers to loss. "I am like a lonely sparrow"
that appeared to be lost (Psalm 102:7 ESV).

Lamentations 1 speaks of Jerusalem as a lonely city after its fall: "Lonely sits the city [Jerusalem] that was [once] full of people! How like a widow she has become. She who was great among the nations!" (v. 1 AMP). It goes on to say, "She has no one to comfort her. All her friends have dealt treacherously with her" (v. 2 AMP). If I can relate to those words and say such things about my life, then I can momentarily use the word *lonely*. In my deepest sorrow, God is there to pick me up, love me, heal me, and restore my life just as he restored Job's life. Job 42:10 tells us that the Lord gave Job twice as much as Job had before he lost everything. He went on to live a long life full of days.

Affirmations

- I trust God. "Though he slay me, yet will I trust Him" (Job 13:15 KJV).
- Nothing on earth can rob me of my love and trust in the Lord Jesus, who brings good friends into my life.
- I repent of wallowing in feelings of loneliness when I have others to call on.
- I refuse to cling to feelings of loneliness.
- I release myself from clinging to feelings of loneliness and look forward to a blessed future in Christ.

24

ANXIETY

"If you then are not able to do the least,
why are you anxious for the rest?"
LUKE 12:26

Anxiety in a person's heart weighs him down,
but an encouraging word brings him joy.
PROVERBS 12:25 NET

In the multitude of my [anxious] thoughts within me,
Your comforts cheer and delight my soul!
PSALM 94:19 AMPC

Meditate

Typically, we're anxious over a threatening event, a "what-if" situation, or fear of the future or outcome of something. We're anxious when we're excessively apprehensive, feeling trapped, or frantic over something real or imagined. I've had clients in the counseling room tell me that their anxiety felt like running a race with no finish line. One client described the feeling as swimming up the Mississippi.

Anxiety is a more physically obvious emotion than worry, which tends to dwell silently on troubles and outcomes. You can overcome anxiety and worry, and a good place to start is by paying attention to your self-talk. Counter your negative inner dialogue with the truth. You have nothing to fear. Jesus, our ultimate therapist, holds the antidote for anxiety. He gives you new inner dialogue to help you. We can be free from the crushing grip of anxious thinking.

It may seem too simplistic to challenge our false thinking with the truth, but it works. Focus on these affirmations.

Affirmations

- I am free from the chains of anxiety through the powerful love of the Lord Jesus, who died to set me free from myself and future judgment.
- No longer will I grind my teeth over unseen events and outcomes. I am released from the inner turmoil that once possessed me.
- I fear nothing as of this day.
- I am a new creation in Christ (2 Corinthians 5:17).
- I totally release myself from the habit of accepting inner turmoil as okay.
- I have the peace of God in me to handle all situations well.
- I'm a courageous and trusting person.
- My loved ones and I are protected by the power of the Holy Spirit.

25

PATIENCE

I waited patiently for the LORD;
and He inclined to me, and heard my cry.
PSALM 40:1

The fruit of the Spirit is love, joy, peace, patience, kindness,
goodness, faithfulness, gentleness, and self-control.
GALATIANS 5:22–23 NET

What credit is it if, when you are beaten for your faults, you
take it patiently? But when you do good and suffer, if you
take it patiently, this is commendable before God.
1 PETER 2:20

Meditate

The Holy Spirit's gift of patience covers a lot of territory.
Frustration, anger, bitterness, and depression are often
products of a lack of patience. But look on the good side.
We could never learn to be patient if there weren't trouble
and hardship in our lives and in the world. To live a
fulfilled life in the Lord, we need the gift of patience in full
operation every day.

Impatience is a close cousin of complaining. When
you feel impatient, watch the things you say. There will be a
complaint in there somewhere because things aren't going
the way you want or need them to. Impatience looms its
head over the tiniest to the biggest things, from an inability
to thread a needle to waiting for a runaway child to return.

The fast pace of technology has increased our feelings of impatience, and patience is becoming a rare skill in the modern world of speed, rush, convenience, and quick results. Recognizing impatience in yourself can open your awareness to what's really going on inside. Within you, waiting to be utilized, are the peace of God, a calm spirit, and all the patience you need. The next time you're tempted to honk at the car in front of you at a green light or snap at a waiter when the food takes too long, stop and remind yourself that you are a person of patience.

We can even become impatient with God when he doesn't answer prayers when we want him to. Patience goes hand in hand with faith. You can never lose your patience. It doesn't go anywhere. Both patience and faith can get pushed aside in the midst of your busy life, but they're in you, right next to the peace of God, as fruit of the Holy Spirit. Faith is patient. Love is patient. A calm and peaceful spirit lives in you. Exercise your patience. Practice patience like you'd practice running or playing the flute. Use the following affirmations to build exemplary patience that's ready for any situation.

Affirmations

- In the name of Jesus, I am a patient person.
- Exemplary patience of the Lord lives in me.
- I don't push patience aside when mistakes happen.
- Within me, waiting to be utilized, are the peace of God, a calm spirit, and all the patience I need.
- In suffering, I am patient.

26

FRUSTRATION

Do not fear, for I am with you; do not be dismayed,
for I am your God. I will strengthen you and help you;
I will uphold you with my righteous right hand.

ISAIAH 41:10 NIV

Meditate

Frustration is like a wet shawl of misery taking advantage of your energy. Frustration steals your sensibility and reasoning abilities.

Frustration and anger are close cousins. When you're working at something for hours and it still doesn't go right, you might want either to cry or to punch something. When you feel frustrated, you are in a place where you could potentially insult and hurt somebody. Frustration often results in arguments and altercations you could easily avoid. When you have a grievance with someone or if you're annoyed with someone or something, call it frustration and don't let it damage your soul.

Late Middle English and Latin translate *frustration* as "deception, in vain" and relate it to injury and harm. Frustration is a harmful thing that can make you sick, so when you feel frustrated, pause immediately and take a long, slow breath. Think of the word *yes* without opening your mouth.[6] If you open your mouth, you may say something you wish you hadn't. With your mouth shut, you

---

6 For more information on the Yes Prayer, read Meditation 41 titled "Blessings of the Yes Prayer."

can't raise your voice, shout, or curse. Allow your shoulders to relax. If it's possible, get away from whatever you're doing or experiencing. Remain still and in a relaxed position for as long as it takes you to calm down.

Imagine Jesus preaching in the synagogue and nobody listening or understanding what he's talking about. Would Jesus pout, grumble, or feel hurt? Jesus had less success teaching than he did working miracles. Did that frustrate him? No. Jesus was fortified with the Holy Spirit, knowledge, and patience, same as you. The miracles of the time would pass away, but his words would live forever.

Within you is enormous wisdom, and you can count on it in frustrating situations. When you repeat the following affirmations, you'll recognize how to control frustration when it looms up in you and how to push it out.

Affirmations

- I do not fall into frustrating situations by taking on more than I know I can handle.
- I will not add to someone else's frustration by trying to talk them out of it or giving advice.
- I am strong in the Lord and do not allow frustration to have any place in my life.
- I stand against frustration with wisdom.
- Frustration doesn't handle me. I handle frustration.
- I recognize frustration as injury and harm, and I reject it.

27

AMBITION

The one who pursues righteousness
and love finds life, bounty, and honor.
PROVERBS 21:21 NET

Meditate

There are two sides to the word *ambition*. One is the selfish
connotation, and the other is selfless. For this meditation,
let's look at the selfless aspect. As a child of God, you have
built in you the desire to share with others the wonderful
things God has done in your life. You want everyone
to know the Lord as you do. This is a selfless ambition.
Ambition always carries with it hard work and dedication.
You want to carry God's love to the world. We do this
everywhere we go.

You're called as an ambassador of God's love.
Your personal life can be your most important message.
Paul wrote to the Thessalonians that they should aspire
to live quietly, to work hard so they would be a good
example to everyone, and to never ask anything of them
(1 Thessalonians 4:11). Our private lives can be a clear
demonstration of our faith and humility.

Ambition requires discipline. Our ambition, though
pure and selfless, always requires inner discipline. We need
our thoughts disciplined to honor God and represent him
for who he is. Paul wrote in Philippians 4:8 that we should
keep our minds on what's true, noble, good, pure, and
lovely. This verse is crucial training for us because if we're

undisciplined, proud, and critical, we'll fall radically short of loving the world into the kingdom of God.

Everything Jesus did when on earth he did with divine, holy love. You and I have that same divine, holy love in us. We bring it out when we train our ambition to reflect God's love with selfless preparation. Paul wrote in 2 Timothy 4:2 that we should preach the gospel and be prepared in season and out of season. We must also "let no one seek his own good, but the good of his neighbor" (1 Corinthians 10:24 ESV).

By far the most important training manual for Christians is 1 Corinthians 13. It's in these words that ambition faces the biggest challenges in life. Paul warns that if I speak and preach beautiful messages without love, I'm just making a lot of noise. My brilliant prophecies and proliferating mean nothing without love. My faith is dust without love. If I give to the poor and die a martyr's death without love, my actions are pointless. Love isn't anxious and easily upset. Love doesn't give up. Love simply can't fail. Let your ambition be this: live and share the power that never fails—God's love in you.

Affirmations

- I train my mind with Philippians 4:8.
- I train my conscience with 1 Corinthians 10:24.
- I train my humility with 1 Thessalonians 4:11.
- I am anointed to live my life in 1 Corinthians 13.
- I love the world as Christ loves the world.

28

MY SHEEP HEAR MY VOICE

"My sheep hear My voice, and I know them, and they
follow Me. And I give them eternal life, and they shall never
perish; neither shall anyone snatch them out of My hand."

JOHN 10:27–28

Meditate

The sheep that the Father gives the Son belong to him. The
sheep (that's us) are obedient and faithful to their one and
only Shepherd (Jesus). His sheep belong to his personal
flock, his family forever. In turn, the sheep are guaranteed
permanent protection. God commits all his resources to
our spiritual care.

Jesus, using the metaphor of a shepherd and
his sheep, was affirming that his children are the ones
who recognize his voice. Nobody else. He's making two
important points here. One, nobody else but his sheep
recognizes his leading. Unbelievers don't hear him because
he isn't their shepherd. In Matthew 16:15–17, Jesus asked
Peter, "Who do you say that I am?" and Peter responded,
"You are the Christ, the Son of the living God." Jesus was
delighted. "Blessed are you, Simon Bar-Jonah," he said, "for
flesh and blood has not revealed this to you, but My Father
who is in heaven." Peter belonged to Jesus' flock and could
hear the truth from God.

When referring to hearing the voice of God, Jesus
said not once but three times in the book of Matthew, "He
who has ears to hear, let him hear!" (11:15; 13:9, 43). What

kind of ears was he talking about? A spiritual relationship with Jesus as our Shepherd, leader, and Messiah opens our spiritual ears to hear without words, which is exactly how we hear the Shepherd's voice.

We hear the voice of God through our study of his Word, sermons, books, Christian friends, counselors, teachers, and our inner sense of God's prompting. Jesus said not only do we hear his voice, but we also know his voice. We have the born-again ears to recognize and hear his voice. Jesus' parable of the sower concludes with "Whoever has, to him more will be given" (13:12). We're getting better at hearing his voice all the time as our faith keeps growing and we keep listening.

Affirmations

- God speaks to me through his Word.
- The Holy Spirit teaches me to listen to the voice of God's leading in my life.
- I recognize when God is leading me.
- I pay careful attention and listen for the leading of the Lord.
- God speaks to me in silence, and I hear him.
- Jesus, my Shepherd, knows who I am and leads me in ways I can understand and follow.
- I am a sheep in the arms of my Shepherd. I will not follow false leaders.

29

I AM ENOUGH

You are complete in Him,
who is the head of all principality and power.
Colossians 2:10

Meditate

If every child of God realized they are complete in Christ,
lacking nothing, how happy we'd be as a universal family.
The world would see us completely differently. We wouldn't
be people who place our unmet needs and insecurities on
the lap of an indifferent world. We'd have no demands on
others to fill what's missing in us. We'd be content. Our
entire approach to life would hold the sheen of confidence.
We'd be what it means to be people of faith.

The negative feeling that we aren't enough is
insidious, evident in faultfinding, habitual dissatisfaction,
bad tempers, and addictive behaviors like overeating, the
use of pornography, and drug and alcohol abuse. The deep-
seated belief that we are not enough is part of low self-
esteem, which indicates nonappreciation and abhorrence
for what we *are*. Feelings of not being enough focus us on
what we think we are and have *not*.

The negative feeling of not being enough can be
mistaken for shyness or humility. In truth, it's ego-driven
self-absorption. The idea that other people have more
talent, brains, good looks, prestige, luck, or personality than
we do is (brace yourself) absolutely true. Just don't stop and
camp at what others have. Open your eyes to the things you

have that are completely yours alone. Stay clear of Public Enemy Number One, which is *comparison*. Put signs up all over where you live, in your car, in your pockets that say, "I don't compare myself with anyone. I am enough."

Your journey of enoughness begins by taking a sheet of paper and writing across the top "I lack nothing." Then write a list of what you honor and respect about yourself. (You'll be adding to this list daily.) Next write down what you're going to honor and accept in others. No more wishing that you had what they have or do what they do. See yourself bringing to the world all that you are in Christ.

Repeat the following affirmations as often as you can because you aren't a wounded bird on a housetop (Psalm 102:7). You haven't missed the boat; you're not missing anything. You have in you absolutely everything you need. You are mighty, beautiful, and strong in the Lord. You are *enough*.

Affirmations

- My God has supplied all my needs according to his riches in Christ Jesus (Philippians 4:19).
- I'm called to be complete in Christ. And so I am.
- I lack nothing. I put a stop to comparing myself to others. I am listening to the truth of who I am in Christ.
- I am loved and appreciated, and I am not missing anything.
- God gives me all I need to fulfill my purpose in life.

30

DESIRE

Delight yourself in the LORD,
and he will give you the desires of your heart.
PSALM 37:4 ESV

One thing I have desired of the LORD, that will I seek: that I may dwell in the house of the LORD all the days of my life, to behold the beauty of the LORD, and to inquire in His temple.
PSALM 27:4

Meditate

To desire is part of our human nature. Desire defines our wants and wishes. There's a distinct separation between your natural wishes and wants and the desires God puts in your heart. Many natural wishes and wants don't have action behind them to make them possible. For example, "I wish I could go on a cruise" is just a wish unless you take steps to make it happen. "I wish I were twenty-one again" is another wish. We use the expression "I wish" all the time, and wishes can be a lot of fun in games, in fairy tales, or for birthday candles. To want isn't much different though it's often connected to our needs: "I want Mary to come back," and "I want Tom to fix the washing machine."

Often when we wish and want, we leave out the aspect of prayer, but we can easily incorporate our desires into our prayer. For instance, turn "I wish I knew where I left my keys" to the prayer "Lord Jesus, please lead me to my keys" and to the affirmation "In the name of Jesus, I can find my keys."

For the child of God, there's holiness in *desire*, especially when we pursue the desires God has placed on our hearts. In Psalm 27:4 David had but one desire, and that was to live where God lives. When a child of God brings a desire to God, it's like an offering of concern and even a longing for God himself. You bring your heart to God's heart with your desire. David didn't write, "One thing I prayed to the Lord for…" No, he said, "One thing I have desired of the LORD." David was accustomed to bringing his desires before the Lord.

Earlier, in Psalm 10:17, he tells God, "O LORD, you will hear the desire of the meek; you will strengthen their heart; you will incline your ear" (NRSVUE).

Your prayers are intensified when preceded by deep desire. Inspired by the Holy Spirit, the more heartfelt your desires, the more heartfelt your prayers. Desire is communion with God on a very passionate level. David's only desire was to live with the Lord. That was the one thing he asked of God. What are your desires?

Affirmations

- I recognize the difference between my wishes and wants and Holy Spirit–inspired desires.
- God hears and answers my Spirit-led desires.
- One thing I desire of God is to behold his beauty and live beside him (Psalm 27:4).
- My desire is to know God more intimately day by day.

31

HOPE

Christ in you, the hope of glory.
COLOSSIANS 1:27

We desire that each one of you show the same diligence to
the full assurance of hope until the end, that you do not
become sluggish, but imitate those who through faith and
patience inherit the promises.
HEBREWS 6:11–12

Meditate

When we use the word *hope* in everyday conversation,
it often conveys a feeling of doubt, such as, "I hope I'll
get there on time," or "I hope I get a raise." The biblical
meaning of the word *hope* contains no doubt. Both the
Old and New Testaments of the Bible translate *hope* as
"confidence," "security," and "being without care." There's no
doubt implied.

The eleventh chapter of Hebrews in the New
Testament begins "Now faith is the substance of things
hoped for, the evidence of things not seen." This verse
implies that there is no doubt with the word *hope*. It is
saying that faith is the substance of that which we are
absolutely confident in, without the tiniest flicker of doubt.

Psalm 31:24 says, "Be of good courage, and He shall
strengthen your heart, all you who hope in the LORD." It is
an encouragement to God's children whose confidence in
him leaves no room for the smallest doubt. Where you see

the word *hope* in the Bible, always translate it to *confidence*, and you'll have the proper meaning.

Affirmations

- I do not use the word *hope* while leaving room for doubt.
- My hope (my confidence) is secure in Christ.
- Christian hope gives me nothing to doubt.
- I am secure in my faith. I affirm that my confidence is solidly fixed in my Lord and Savior, Jesus Christ.
- I am confident in who I am in Christ and am secure in all his promises to me.
- Nothing can sneak into my head to make me doubt that my faith is anything but real because it is substantial.

32

I AM CONTENT

Not that I speak in regard to need,
for I have learned in whatever state I am, to be content.
PHILIPPIANS 4:11

Let your conduct be without covetousness; be content
with such things as you have. For He Himself has said,
"I will never leave you nor forsake you."
HEBREWS 13:5

Some trust in chariots, and some in horses;
but we will remember the name of the LORD our God.
PSALM 20:7

Meditate

The greatness of God reduces my complaints to dust. Every day I teach myself to be content. I remind myself of Job in the Bible, who woke up one day to find his whole world suddenly torn apart. God must have known Job really well to trust him through incredible loss and suffering. Without warning and in the space of a few days, Satan brought terrible things down on Job. They came one after another like bullets, including the losses of his children, home, property, land, servants, crops, animals, and even his own physical health when he was covered in ugly and painful boils from head to toe.

The story of Job is a classic for every child of God because through this man, we see with dramatic clarity the lower value of earthly possessions compared to the riches of knowing God. Job lost his children along with all his riches and honor. He lost everything except three friends, who made his situation worse.

All through the Bible we're told to be strong and courageous (Joshua 1:6), to overcome (Revelation 2:7), to rise above (Psalm 24:7), to be empowered by faith and the Spirit of God (Acts 1:8). From Moses to Paul, we're admonished not to put our faith in possessions or in relationships but in God alone. This is the key to contentment. With or without, we live abundant lives in him.

"The thief does not come except to steal, and to kill, and to destroy. I have come that they [you] may have life, and that they [you] may have it more abundantly" (John 10:10).

Affirmations

- I enjoy the abundant blessings of God every day.
- I put no stock in what the world says I lack and continue to affirm the abundant life God has given me.
- I'm content in wealth and in poverty.
- Jesus came to give me abundant life, and being content in all things assures that.
- Some trust in riches and some in people, but I will trust in the name of the Lord my God.
- I take the eternal, unchanging arm of love, and I am content.

33

THE HAPPY CHILD OF GOD

Happy are the people
whose God is the LORD!
PSALM 144:15

Meditate

The nineteenth-century theologian Charles Spurgeon said, "It is not how much we have, but how much we enjoy that makes happiness."[7] This is different from how our culture defines happiness, which to them depends upon circumstances, situations, or someone else, making it fleeting and fragile. That's why many people are always chasing an elusive happiness. Without God, happiness is a dependent commodity with prerequisites and conditions. For the child of God, happiness is God himself. We aren't victims of life's ups and downs. God is our happiness, and choosing to be happy is choosing him. He gives us the skill to choose happiness on a consistent basis.

Happiness depends on our inner dialogue. Look at what you tell yourself during the day. Tell yourself how good you feel, how good life is; look for what's beautiful and delightful. Read Philippians 4:8 and make a conscious, heartfelt effort to choose happy thoughts.

Happiness, joy, and peace belong to God. I remember a particularly difficult time in my life when I felt my world had fallen apart and could never be put back

---

7   Charles H. Spurgeon, *John Ploughman's Talk* (Pensacola, FL: Chapel Library, 2016), 8, https://www.chapellibrary.org/pdf/books/jpta.pdf.

together again. I sat on my sofa, tears dripping down my chin, and I suddenly started to sing. From out of my mouth came a little shaky voice: "God is so good, God is so good, he's so good to me." I must have sat there for over an hour singing away. In my despair something happy and joyful came out of me.

Happiness like that can't be explained. Happiness and joy are closely related. Happiness is an outward flow of emotion, and joy is the Holy Spirit's stability coming from a well inside us, not outside us. Ask yourself these words every day: *Are you happy?* And always, no matter how you feel, answer yes. Everything you do corresponds to what you tell yourself. Notice how different you feel when you say yes to joyfulness. You don't need circumstances or another person to experience the happiness that comes from the joy of the Lord within you. Your world can fall apart, and you can emerge from the rubble singing. Your soul hears those words; your brain hears those words. Your body hears those words, and God hears those words.

Affirmations

- I now stop waiting around for happiness to show up.
- I will remember that happiness is a choice.
- I will stop thinking I'm entitled to what I want in order to be full of joy.
- Happiness is a skill I can teach myself.
- I am happy.

34

GOD KNOWS ME

"The very hairs of your head are all numbered."
MATTHEW 10:30

You created my inmost being;
you knit me together in my mother's womb.
PSALM 139:13 NIV

Meditate

The only one who really knows me in this life is God. He
knit me together in my mother's womb. God was closer to
me than my mother was. Nobody else was there except God.
God knows exactly how he created me. He knew where
to place the hairs on my head and counted them. There is
nothing about me he doesn't know, including my personality,
intellect, and gifts. God knows my personality and doesn't
ask me to be like anyone else. My life since the moment
I was born has been under his scrutiny. He knows how I
think and what interests me. He knows my talents and my
dreams. He knows my past and my future, and he loves me
unconditionally. No human being can make these claims.

Is it a good thing that nobody knows me as God
knows me? The answer is yes because God has created me
for himself and then for the life he gives me. I'm alive and
well in the world, but the world is not alive and well in me.
My permanent home is in God. I'm a temporary resident of
the world. He's given me a deep, deep love for his world as
his child, but I'm not a child of the world.

The world has no idea who I am, and the universe has no idea who I am, not caring who I am or what I'm up to. The universe has no brain. God created the universe, and he created me as a human in his image (Genesis 1:27). God is spirit, and his spirit is the essence and reality of my existence. God loves everything about me because when he looks at me, he sees Jesus, his Son (his image).

Jesus said we can do nothing without him (John 15:5), and this should give us a clue about our limitations. If I can't do anything without him and he lives in me by his Spirit, the real me is only in operation when the Holy Spirit is my source. This is good to know when our egos jump in and tell us we're the source behind all the good we do. God knows you love him. He knows you want his will for your life. Your heavenly Father knows who you are, and knowing you, he loves you.

Affirmations

- God knows the real me and loves me exactly as I am.
- I am the apple of God's eye.
- God knows me better than anyone, and I'm secure in knowing he knows me.
- God's love for me is my most treasured possession.
- I can be at peace when others don't understand me because I'm perfectly understood by God.
- I'm fearfully and wonderfully made (Psalm 139:14).
- I'm distinct and amazing in Christ.

35

LAUGHTER

[There is] a time to cry and a time to laugh.
ECCLESIASTES 3:4 NLT

Our mouth was filled with laughter, And our tongue with singing. Then they said among the nations, "The LORD has done great things for them."
PSALM 126:2

"He will once again fill your mouth with laughter and your lips with shouts of joy."
JOB 8:21 NLT

Meditate

Have you laughed today? Many medical studies have long shown the health benefits of laughter. Laughter is good for your heart, immune system, blood pressure, and nervous system; it relaxes your body and reduces pain. Laughter releases endorphins, the same hormone that exercise releases. We need those endorphins. Studies have shown that people who laugh heartily every day may live longer than those who hardly ever laugh. Laughter also affects the quality of your life.

My sister and brother-in-law have been married for over thirty years, and you'll always find them laughing together. They have developed laughter habits without trying. They appreciate and admire each other, which their humor and laughter make obvious. Demanding careers, tragedy, and major health issues, including a life-threatening bout with cancer, haven't dampened their sense of humor. Their humor reaches into the atmosphere around them, and if there's chaos in the air, their laughter will diminish it.

Jesus had a sense of humor when he was on earth. I think of the crowd listening to him teach and laughing hilariously when he said, "I tell you, it is easier for a camel to go through the eye of a needle" (Matthew 19:24 NIV). How could a camel get through the eye of a needle? Those listening must have thought that was hilarious.

A good hearty belly laugh is real medicine. Some things are just so hysterical that you laugh so hard the tears clink on the floor. A good chuckle is fine, as well as a snicker or a friendly chortle, but the belly laugh is the king of laughs. Make sure a week doesn't go by without a good belly laugh.

You don't have to be happy to laugh. Something just has to strike you as funny. Today find at least three things that make you laugh.

Affirmations

- I make sure to laugh every day.
- I find many things in life hilarious.
- I don't laugh at anything derisive or mean.
- I never hurt someone's feelings by laughing at them.
- I never tease someone by laughing at them.
- I inspire laughter around me.
- I laugh at trouble. I don't fear it.

36

TAKING A BREAK FROM LIFE

He makes me to lie down in green pastures;
He leads me beside the still waters.
PSALM 23:2

What has man for all his labor, and for the striving of his
heart with which he has toiled under the sun?
ECCLESIASTES 2:22

Meditate

How worn out do we have to get before we stop what we're
doing and take a break? If you're starting a business, going
to school, or making ends meet with two or three jobs, you
probably don't have time for breaks. You may be a person
like I used to be, working around the clock. I had writing
deadlines, a counseling and fitness clinic to run, teaching,
travel, and family to take care of.

Then the inevitable happened. I overworked myself.
It's called burnout.

The pressure of our workload can be so
overwhelming that taking breaks seems like a waste of
time. The National Institute for Occupational Safety and
Health has found in studies that not taking regular breaks
from work and stressful situations produces health risks,
increasing the money workers and their employers spend
on health care as a result.[8] Overworking weakens the

---

8 "Work and Fatigue," Centers for Disease Control and Prevention, last
updated March 2, 2023, https://www.cdc.gov/niosh/topics/fatigue/.

immune system, can lead to sleep disorders, and decreases mental acumen.

If you're thinking a month on the beach in Málaga or a year in the woods of Vermont sounds good, you can actually generate the same peaceful rest for your body and soul by regularly sitting down in silence for twenty minutes alone with God. Find the most spiritually restful activity you can think of to let go of every duty, obligation, and accompanying pressure. It can be as simple as lying on the grass while looking at the sky, getting a massage, going for a swim, or taking a cozy nap. If you bring your workload, troubles, and pressure along with you, you aren't resting. You're sabotaging your time for peace and regeneration.

When we're worn to the bone and still don't schedule moments of rest, hear Jesus speak gently to your heart, *Come to me with your heavy labors and stress, and I'll give you the rest you must have* (Matthew 11:28, author's paraphrase).

Here's an idea: Why not take a soul vacation with Jesus? Schedule a day or a week or an hour for just you and Jesus. No need to head for Corfu when you have a space in your house, apartment, parked car, cabin, or yurt where you can rest and breathe in the sweet presence of God.

Affirmations

- I honor God by taking breaks from myself.
- Jesus calls me to give him my heavy burdens, and so I do.
- I am more productive because I take breaks and rest.
- I love to take my soul vacations with Jesus.

37

GOD'S FRIEND

Jesus answered him, "If anyone loves me, he will keep my word, and my Father will love him, and we will come to him and make our home with him."

JOHN 14:23 ESV

There is a friend who sticks closer than a brother.

PROVERBS 18:24 ESV

Meditate

Friendship with God is the greatest thing you can experience in life. The Lord's loyal kindness and love never cease; his compassion never ends. They are new and fresh every morning; his faithfulness never fades and never exhausts itself (Lamentations 3:21–2). And he's our friend! God called Abraham "my friend" (Isaiah 41:8), and Moses was so close to God that he talked face-to-face with the Lord (Exodus 33:11).

Our friendship with God begins with the word *reconciliation*, which in Greek means "change" or "exchange." It's when we make a change from our ways to God's ways. This takes getting to know his ways, of course, and this is a lifelong job. Even in eternity, where there is no sin or pain, we'll be learning about the ways of God ad infinitum. Eternity isn't long enough to know everything there is to know about God. But how wonderful it is to daily caress what we do know.

Your love for the Lord pulls adoration out of you. Your love pulls deep loyalty out of you. God wants loyal friends, friends who are faithful and at peace with who God is and his desires. Our friendship with God is a supernatural revelation. Being a best friend of God is not like being friends with a person, which requires equality. You are close friends with human friends when there's no superiority and no one dominating the other. You don't obey your human friend. However, Jesus said we are his friends if we do what he commands us (John 15:14), and that's not like a relationship between humans. Don't compare your human friendships to your friendship with God. Friendship with God is exchanging the old you for the shiny brand new you. "Therefore, if anyone is in Christ, he is a new creation; old things have passed away; behold, all things have become new" (2 Corinthians 5:17).

Affirmations

- No human being can be a friend to me like God.
- I am a friend of God and loyal to him in all my ways.
- I choose to live my life daily as God's friend.
- I do not settle for shallow faith that finds it difficult to obey the Lord.
- All that is within me blesses the name of Jesus, who is my friend.
- Jesus is faithful and will never walk out on me.
- I am faithful to Jesus and will never walk out on him.

38

I AM NOT AFRAID

Do not be afraid of sudden terror,
nor of trouble from the wicked when it comes.

"'Therefore do not fear, O My servant Jacob,' says the LORD,
'Nor be dismayed, O Israel; For behold, I will save you from
afar, and your seed from the land of their captivity. Jacob
shall return, have rest and be quiet, and no one shall make
him afraid.'"

JEREMIAH 30:10

"'Do not be afraid of the king of Babylon, of whom you
are afraid; do not be afraid of him,' says the LORD, 'for I am
with you, to save you and deliver you from his hand.'"

JEREMIAH 42:11

Meditate

Sometimes the thing we're afraid to do is the very thing
we should do. In Jeremiah, we're told that God gave the
Israelites a choice to make that required trust in him.
They could stay in the kingdom of Judah, which had been
battered by the Babylonian conquest, with no walls to
protect their cities and no trained army. Egypt, on the other
hand, thrived in luxury. Through Jeremiah the prophet,
God warned them not to go to Egypt. God promised he
would protect them and provide for them in Judah if they
would stay. He promised to be with them and save them
from the king of Babylon, but they only pretended to listen

to him. They packed up and took themselves to Egypt because Egypt looked better to them than Judah. In no time, they were devoured (Jeremiah 40–44).

If God's people had trusted the word of the Lord, they would have flourished and prospered in the promised land. Because they were afraid and didn't trust God, they perished. They chose what looked good to them instead of what was good. They were so afraid that their hearts were hardened. Don't be afraid of the unknown. Don't be afraid of making a mistake. Trust God and enlarge your world.

Affirmations

- I am not afraid. God is with me.
- I stop being afraid that God's promises aren't for me.
- I am not afraid of anything that threatens me.
- I cannot be threatened.
- I am not helpless when I face danger.
- I stop thinking I'm not good enough for God to take care of me.
- I will obey the word of the Lord and not be afraid.
- I trust the Lord to help me go on the right path.
- I am not afraid of people.
- I am not afraid of failure.
- I reject and renounce fear in my life in any shape or form.

39

FILLED WITH THE HOLY SPIRIT

[The disciples] were all filled with the Holy Spirit
and began to speak the word of God courageously.

ACTS 4:31 NET

"It is not you who speak, but the Holy Spirit."

MARK 13:11

When He [Jesus] had said this, He breathed on them,
and said to them, "Receive the Holy Spirit."

JOHN 20:22

Meditate

Throughout human history, the men and women who did
great deeds for God and humanity were filled with God's
Holy Spirit. In the Bible, from Abraham to the disciples,
we see the Holy Spirit. The power of the Holy Spirit filled
human beings so they could fulfill the will of almighty God
and express his love and power on earth.

Today we are the ones anointed and carrying the
power of the Holy Spirit in the world. The Abrahams,
Davids, Daniels, Jeremiahs, Ezekiels, Pauls, Peters, and Johns
are here right now in us, God's Holy Spirit–filled children.
The same Spirit who raised Christ from the dead dwells in
you (Romans 8:11). The same Spirit who brought down the
walls of Jericho for Joshua lives in you. The same Spirit who
led Moses, Elijah, and the apostle Paul dwells in you.

You were born for this hour because the greatest
gift ever given to live in the hearts of humankind lives in

you. Jesus told his disciples the Holy Spirit would be in us (teaching, guiding, and empowering us) forever (John 14:16–17). Jesus gives us his authority to make known that the kingdom of God is here and now (Matthew 10:7). He gave us instructions to go into all the world and preach the gospel to all nations (Mark 16:15), heal the sick, raise the dead, cleanse the leper, and drive out demons. "You have received freely," he said, "so give freely" (Matthew 10:8 NIrV). We can only do these holy things with the Holy Spirit in control of our lives.

Affirmations

- I am filled with the same Spirit who raised Christ from the dead.
- In me is the source of life itself.
- The Holy Spirit empowers me to live beyond my spiritual intentions and my own ideas about God.
- Greater is the Holy Spirit in me than any intrusion of the world.
- I am sealed with the Holy Spirit of promise.
- I am owned, protected, and validated by the Holy Spirit (Ephesians 1:13–14).
- I am filled with the Holy Spirit to be, do, and go where he sends me.
- I have the power of the Holy Spirit in me.

40

PRAYER IN STILLNESS

Be still, and know that I am God.
Psalm 46:10

Thy kingdom come,
Thy will be done in earth, as it is in heaven.
Matthew 6:10 KJV

Meditate

The hours you spend in prayer are the closest you can get to heaven on earth. In the Lord's Prayer, Jesus taught us to pray, "Thy kingdom come...in earth, as it is heaven." Your doorway to heaven on earth is to bring yourself to prayer. It's amazing to think that the Creator of all also sits privately with his children, listens, and responds. The apostle James said we have not because we ask not (James 4:2–3), and asking is a large component of prayer along with intercession, praise, supplication, worship, adoration, thanksgiving, and confession. In prayer our will stops, and his begins.

You create your own passageway to heaven on earth in your prayer life. Get alone with God for a special period of prayer today. Pray in your bedroom, kitchen, backyard, garage, rooftop, basement, or storage room. Find a special quiet place that's all yours where you meet with God for prayer. Make it your sacred space where you go every day to be alone with God. I know you can pray all during the day; that is, you talk to God, and that's what we do when we love him. Each moment is fueled by the hours you spend alone with him, just the two of you.

An important component of prayer is time you spend just being quiet in the presence of God. Prayer is a time to talk to God and a time to be still. In the stillness, we ask for nothing, talk about nothing, and just sit in silence with him. In the quiet, our minds and bodies settle down, and we release all concerns to simply sit. Stillness is one of God's finest gifts to us if we receive it. I suggest sitting in silence with God every day by setting a timer for the length of time you want. I consider twenty minutes an average amount of time. Twice a day for twenty minutes each time will help in your other times of prayer. You'll find your regular prayer life change and become deeper and filled with more spiritual insight and awareness. This time alone with God in silence opens the door of your heart to find yourself in a space with God where there's no space for anything else. The peace of God that passes your understanding envelops and invites you to put everything aside and just be still.

Prayer time should include a time for words and a time for silence.

Affirmations

- I love my time of stillness in prayer.
- I love being still with God.
- My time in stillness with God is a priority in my life.
- Stillness brings me into the presence of God, and I am secure, enriched, and fortified.

41

BLESSINGS OF THE YES PRAYER

Trust in the LORD with all your heart, and do not lean on your own understanding. In all your ways acknowledge him, and he will make straight your paths.

PROVERBS 3:5–6 ESV

Meditate

Let's imagine something has just happened that you didn't want to happen. Name it. Ordinarily you'd get upset. You might get angry, curse, bite your mouth. The Yes Prayer slides right over those reactions and says yes to the situation.[9] Let's say Jane drops a vase that she inherited from her grandmother. It's valuable and well loved, and it's in pieces scattered on the floor. I use this example because Jane has a few choices. She can become terribly upset, cry, scream, blame someone—or she can say yes.

By saying yes, you're telling the situation that it has no control over you. Saying yes shuts down the emotional powerhouse taking over in you and allows you to assess the situation and respond rationally rather than react instinctively. Here's how you can say yes:

1. When an upsetting situation or event occurs, immediately say yes to it.

2. Take some deep breaths and change your body position.

---

9 The Yes Prayer is inspired by the Welcoming Prayer developed by Father Thomas Keating.

3. Pray. Give the situation over to the Lord completely.

4. Speak aloud Romans 8:28. "For those who love God and are called to his purpose, all things work together for good." Sit with the words for as long as you can.

5. Envision a creative response. What can you do to make this situation work for you? This is solution time. (Sweep up the mess, call the mechanic, text your brother.)

6. Here is the best part. Once you've finished the previous steps and you're feeling calm and more assured that all things really do work for the best, see where the gift is in the situation. There's a gift in it for you. Find it.

7. Say yes one more time. Notice how good you feel.

Affirmations

- I'm in training to conquer emotional reactions when things happen that I don't want to happen.
- I say yes to troublesome events that occur instead of reacting emotionally.
- I turn to the truth in upsetting situations, knowing all things work together for good.
- Speaking yes to an upsetting situation or event diminishes its power over my emotions and my mind.
- I give negativity no control over me.

42

THE EYES AND EARS OF GOD

Does he who fashioned the ear not hear?
Does he who formed the eye not see?
PSALM 94:9 NIV

"The eyes of the LORD are toward the righteous,
and His ears attend to their prayer."
1 PETER 3:12 NASB

Meditate

We can recognize the beauty in a blossoming tree, a rose, or a butterfly, but in this meditation, we're going to look at the beauty that lives within us. Beauty recognizes beauty. Beauty appreciates beauty. God's love is beautiful, and beauty is from God. All things in heaven and on earth are created by him, and he said they are good. How deeply do we probe within us to recognize and appreciate the beauty in us and the world?

If I were to ask you what's happening in the world today, what would your answer be? The evil, chaos, and turmoil of the world are easy to see. None of us are blind to the nightmare of war, disease, or political corruption. You have spiritual eyes and ears to see and hear God (Matthew 13:9). What was he talking about when he said, "Blessed are your eyes for they see"? (v. 16).

Jesus offers us the gift of seeing and hearing through his eyes and ears. This means reaching beyond our natural insight to look at the world, your life, and everyone else's life to spiritually find beauty and love in the world, your life, and everyone else's life. Isaiah exclaimed how the Lord gave him beauty for ashes in Isaiah 61:3. He also saw beauty in the feet of those who bring God's truth (Isaiah 52:7). Isaiah saw feet as beautiful! Paul repeated this in Romans 10:15.

When the prophet Samuel was commissioned by the Lord to anoint a king in Israel, God told Samuel not to look at outward appearance, which can be deceitful. God explained that he doesn't see as humans see, "for man looks at the outward appearance, but the LORD looks at the heart" (1 Samuel 16:7).

This week, find something beautiful in everything. Look with your spiritual eyes and see that he has even put his love in what you perceive as ugly.

Affirmations

- I see with the loving eyes of God.
- The Holy Spirit within me helps me appreciate the world with God's eyes.
- The world and its darkness do not control my vision of what is beautiful to God.
- I have spiritual eyes and ears to see and listen for the beauty in people.
- I am beautiful to God.
- I no longer dwell on what's wrong in my life. I now look for what is beautiful in my life.

43

HUMILITY

The high and lofty One who inhabits eternity, the Holy One, says this: I live in that high and holy place where those with contrite, humble spirits dwell; and I refresh the humble and give new courage to those with repentant hearts.

ISAIAH 57:15 TLB

The man Moses was very humble,
more than all men who were on the face of the earth.

NUMBERS 12:3

Meditate

When you think of a great world leader, does an image of a truly humble person come to mind? Are the great leaders of history examples of humility for us today? How about leadership in more everyday circumstances—pastors, teachers, HOA board members, CEOs of companies, parents? It should stagger each of us to think of the man Moses, unquestionably one of the greatest human leaders in all of human history, and know that God called him the humblest man on earth.

How did Moses get that way? How did a man highly educated as an adopted son of Pharaoh in the most powerful kingdom on earth become the humblest man on earth? How did a man leading a rebellious nation of slaves to freedom become humble and not despotic? How did a shepherd (with a speech impediment) do it? He lived as a shepherd for forty years after fleeing Egypt. As we study the life of Moses, there is but one answer to his humility, and that is simply this: Moses loved God.

There isn't a haughty soul in heaven. There isn't a proud soul in heaven, a self-serving, angry, overworked, or unscrupulous man, woman, child, or angel in heaven. Isaiah 57:15 says everyone in heaven is humble and goes on to say God will help us in our humility. The relationship Moses had with God was one that humbled Moses and kept him humble. He saw God for who he is, and Moses saw himself for who he was. He didn't think himself more or less valuable than anyone else, and when there was rebellion against him and, worse, when they constructed a golden calf to worship, Moses reacted as Jesus did with the money changers in the temple (Matthew 21:12–17). The only road to humility has to be intimacy with God, where he silently and secretly makes us like him.

Affirmations

- I do not think of myself as any more valuable to God than anyone else is.
- I am willing to deny myself comforts and pleasures for the sake of others.
- I renounce and reject pride.
- I am humbled before God, and I have no high opinion of myself.
- God knows me for who I am, and I receive all accolades from him.
- I am a kind and generous leader.

44

I GUARD MY SOUL

Thorns and snares are in the way of the crooked;
whoever guards his soul will keep far from them.
PROVERBS 22:5 ESV

"What does it benefit a person to gain the whole world,
and forfeit his soul? For what could a person give in
exchange for his soul?"
MARK 8:36–37 NASB

"Don't be afraid of those who kill the body but can't kill the
soul. Instead, be afraid of the one who can destroy both
body and soul in hell."
MATTHEW 10:28 CEB

Meditate

What does it mean to love the Lord our God with all
our heart, soul, and mind? The soul is our intellect, our
emotions, and our will. While the mind here is our frame
of mind or our attitudes, the intellect of the soul is how
and what we think. The Hebrew word for "soul" is *nephesh*,
which means "breath of." Our souls are literally alive by his
breath. Your soul and heart have similar elements but are
not the same. *Heart* in Hebrew, *leval*, refers to conscience,
beliefs, moral character, intentions, desires. Jesus clearly
differentiated heart and soul.

We're held accountable for the matters of the soul
and heart. Jesus gave an all-inclusive order. We are to love
God with all our intellect, emotions, will, conscience,

beliefs, moral character, intentions, desires, passion, and thought life.

Guard your soul. Speak these affirmations to become more aware of the life of your soul.

Affirmations

- I put a guard on my soul. I will not allow my soul to be tainted by the lure of the world.
- I put a guard on my soul, my intellect, my emotions, and my will.
- I guard my soul by living a life of prayer (praying without ceasing).
- I guard my soul by disciplining the words of my mouth.
- I will not allow soul-damaging words to escape from my lips.
- I will not allow soul-damaging activities in my daily life.
- I keep sacred my daily set-apart time in silence with Jesus so he can do a work in me without my interrupting with wordiness.
- I guard my soul against unwise, ungodly choices that wound and destroy.
- I choose to bless the Lord with my soul.
- I guard my soul to bless the Lord.

45

I RESIST TEMPTATION

Since he [Jesus] himself suffered when he was tempted,
he is able to help those who are tempted.
HEBREWS 2:18 NET

All men are tempted. There is no man that lives that
can't be broken down, provided it is the right temptation,
put in the right spot.
HENRY WARD BEECHER, *PROVERBS FROM PLYMOUTH PULPIT*

Meditate

Learning to resist temptation is something we do all our
lives. Some temptations take us by surprise. That's why we
need to be on guard to recognize what's going on in our
hearts and minds. Just as Adam looked at the fruit in Eve's
hand and thought, *Hmm, that looks good*, and took a big
bite, you and I can be duped into thinking something that
looks good is okay when, clearly, it's not.

Temptations appear first in our minds. The chocolate
cheesecake is not tempting you; it's what you tell yourself
about the chocolate cheesecake that's tempting you. The
same is true of all temptation. Whatever you're telling
yourself to do, say, or take that is wrong and inappropriate,
resist by changing what you're telling yourself. God gives
you the insight and strength to resist. John writes in 1 John
2:16 that "everything in the world—the lust of the flesh, the
lust of the eyes, and the pride of life—comes not from the
Father but from the world" (NIV).

The temptations we face include the temptation to control, avoid, be hypervigilant, lose our temper, oversleep, manipulate others, overeat, overwork, abuse substances, lie, cheat, steal—add your own to the list.

When we give in to temptation, it's due to our acting out our inner self-centered ego talk. Your ego is the self-centered part of you that sees yourself as the most important person in the world and believes you should have and do whatever you want. Your ego will always tell you it's okay to do what you should not do and gives you a reason, like *nobody cares*, *you'll show them*, or *life and people owe you*.

The key to overcoming temptation is to listen to what you're telling yourself at that moment. Oppose it with what love is telling you. The love of God will never hurt you or tell you to hurt someone. Dare to build a new, positive neural pathway in your brain by affirming that you're spiritually equipped to manage self-centered drives and that you'll not permit self-centered, ego-driven thinking to be master of the life that belongs to God.

Affirmations

- I submit my thought life to God.
- I refuse to allow my ego to destroy my life.
- I have the power within me to resist temptation.
- I can say no to my ego and self-centered drives.
- I will not be a victim of ignorance.
- Greater is the Holy Spirit in me than my ego and all the temptations in the world.

46

STRONG

He gives power to the weak,
and to those who have no might He increases strength.

ISAIAH 40:29

Meditate

The apostle Paul gave us the spiritual remedy for human weakness (Ephesians 6:10). He told us to take hold of the infinite strength of God within us. He spelled out what God does with human weakness. God goes beyond human capabilities and gives strength where there's no spiritually anointed power.

Physical prowess and mental and emotional fortitude without God are finite human efforts. We can be courageous without God and tackle feats requiring physical skill, stamina, and prowess. In fact, we tend to admire people who can do these things. We make heroes of them and try to emulate them. But inside you is a power greater than your human heroes who may only use natural abilities. You're supernaturally enabled to move mountains. With God in you, everything is possible. You can't make that claim without him. We have the spiritual strength to do it all; we can conquer hatred, defeat, pain, and suffering. Your ego-driven ambitions are a thing of the past.

It takes courage to step out of spiritual ignorance because it can be so appealing. Hold on tight to "Let the weak say, 'I am strong'" (Joel 3:10) because your true strength is from inside the secret passageways of your spirit where God has made a home. You can try to be strong, but strength is not a matter of trying. It's a matter of being.

When we look at the strongest men and women in the Bible, we can see most of them were weak to begin with. Look at Gideon, David, Jeremiah, and even Mary, the mother of Jesus. They were simple people without false pretenses or exalted egos. Not one started out as a mighty man or woman before the Spirit of the Lord got hold of them. The following affirmations based on God's promises are true statements about yourself. Take your time speaking them aloud.

Affirmations

- I'm much stronger than I realize. Within me is an endless source of strength.
- I'm strong in the Lord and in the power of his might (Ephesians 6:10).
- The strength in me continues to grow because it is God's strength in me.
- I am delivered from telling myself I'm weak, stupid, or in any way inferior.
- God prepares the day ahead for me, reminding me to affirm that I'm strong.
- Greater is the power of the Holy Spirit in me than all my human fears, worries, and emotional responses to challenges.
- I am no longer intimidated by people or things that used to make me feel inferior.

47

THE WHOLE ARMOR OF GOD

That you may know…what is the exceeding greatness of His power toward us who believe, according to the working of His mighty power.

EPHESIANS 1:18–19

Meditate

Paul spoke with great urgency when he admonished the Christians at Ephesus to clothe themselves with "the whole armor of God" (Ephesians 6:11). Paul referred to Christians as armed soldiers positioned for battle wearing the helmet of salvation, the shield of faith, the breastplate of right standing with God, and the belt of truth. Paul taught that a Christian fitted with the whole armor of God is now ready to wage war with the enemy of God and win.

He reminded the Ephesian Christians and every Christian ever to live that we don't wrestle against flesh and blood but "against principalities, against powers, against the rulers of the darkness of this age, against spiritual hosts of wickedness in the heavenly places" (v. 12).

If we wear God's spiritual armor and wield spiritual weapons against an army we can't see, we had better be supernaturally trained. No soldier goes to war without training, and you and I are in God's boot camp for life.

Look at James 4:7, which ends with "Resist the devil, and he will flee from you" (NIV). That seems simple compared to Ephesians 6, but it's all the same battle. The first part of James 4:7 is the key to our victory in battle with the devil: "Submit yourselves, then, to God." A fully armored Christian is a fully submitted one. Your supernatural power is to be totally submitted to God before making a move. The same verse in God's Word Translation reads, "Place yourselves under God's authority." His authority is what you carry under your armor.

Are you submitted to weaknesses and sins, or are you submitted to God? With whose authority do you face your battles? Do as Jesus did in the wilderness when tempted by the devil. He took up his sword and blasted Satan with the Word (Matthew 4:1–11). Speak your affirmations aloud daily and triumph over the attacks of the devil both outwardly and inwardly.

Affirmations

- I am submitted solely and wholly to God (James 4:7).
- I wear the spiritual armor of a strong, undefeated child of God (Ephesians 6:11).
- My shield of faith extinguishes the flaming arrows of the Evil One (Ephesians 6:16).
- I wear the impenetrable helmet worn by every child of God in the name of Jesus Christ (Ephesians 6:10; Philippians 2:10).
- In the name of Jesus, I proclaim my life and the lives of my loved ones blessed, healed, and in right standing with God (Acts 16:31).
- I am fearless. No evil can penetrate God's armor (1 John 4:18).

48

REJOICE

Rejoice in the Lord always. Again I will say, rejoice!
PHILIPPIANS 4:4

This is the day the LORD has made;
we will rejoice and be glad in it.
PSALM 118:24

Meditate

The word *rejoice* appears in the Bible almost two hundred times. Paul uses the word *rejoice* nine times in his letter to the Philippians. *Rejoice* means to show great joy, so when we rejoice, we are actually joy-ing. We're turning the noun *joy* into the verb *rejoice*.

The spiritual state of joy resides deep within us. Being joyful and rejoicing are not the same thing our culture defines as being happy. A feeling of happiness is a response to something; it's a way of reacting. "Sunshine makes me happy," or "I'll be happy when I finish cleaning the garage." "When you eat the labor of your hands, you shall be happy" (Psalm 128:2). Joy lives deep within us and needs nothing to react to. Joy simply is. Contentment, assurance, and peace are outpourings of a joyful heart.

Joy is not a reaction. It's a state of being deep within us where the Holy Spirit infuses our human spirit. The troubles and tragedies of life can muffle our spirit of joy, but joy is lodged in our soul no matter how faint. We build and enlarge our joy with love for God and trust in his love and perfect will.

To rejoice is not an action we conjure up from outside ourselves. You and I, as born-again children of God, have all nine fruit of the Holy Spirit within us. Joy is a fruit of the Holy Spirit (Galatians 5:22–23). To rejoice is to release the joy of Jesus (Nehemiah 8:10) that already lives in us. Rejoicing is an intimate partnership with Jesus, the Holy Spirit, the angels, and all of heaven, where there is rejoicing going on without end. We build and enlarge our joy with our love for God and our trust in who he is and who we are in him. Joy creates positive neural pathways in the brain. Joy is as eternal as God is eternal, and it's his joy that gives the world a glimpse of heaven. Breathe in the joy of the Lord as you read slowly and listen to the words you're speaking in the affirmations that follow.

Affirmations

- The Bible says the godly will rejoice in the Lord (Psalm 64:10), and that's me. I rejoice in the Lord always.
- My loving Jesus gives me so much joy I must share it.
- I exude joy.
- My life is flowing with the joy of the Lord, and I rejoice continuously.
- I can't help but rejoice in God.
- I'm so filled with love. How could I not rejoice?
- Rejoicing depends upon nothing outside of me. It comes from within me.
- Yes, I will rejoice in the Lord all the days of my life.

49

I AM GIVING

Give unto the LORD the glory due to His name;
worship the LORD in the beauty of holiness.

PSALM 29:2

"Bring all the tithes into the storehouse, that there may be
food in My house, and try Me now in this," says the LORD
of hosts, "If I will not open for you the windows of heaven
and pour out for you such blessing that there will not be
room enough to receive it."

MALACHI 3:10

I will give You thanks in the great assembly;
I will praise You among many people.

PSALM 35:18

Meditate

You are giving. It's who you are. You could answer your
phone with "Hello, Giving Person here." Start thinking
of yourself as the giving person you are. Scripture speaks
of giving in many more ways than just through material
things. Starting with tithing. Your 10 percent to the Lord's
work is giving. It's not paying for something because you're
not buying something; you're giving. In ancient times, a
tithe was like a 10 percent tax on income or property to
support the temple, which, in turn, supported the people.

You are giving in a thousand ways. When you study
the Word, you are giving of yourself to being edified. When
you give your attention to God's instruction, you're giving

blessing and anointing. When you give your strength, your goods, your kindness, your thoughtfulness, your love, it's the very presence and wonder of God in you. You give your praise and your worship to God and your godly integrity to the world. You give your wisdom and your sense of humor. Everything in you as a child of God is giving because everything about God is giving.

Affirmations

- I love who I am in God.
- I love how the Holy Spirit opens doors for giving.
- I don't resent giving. I rejoice in it.
- I love that I have the gift of discernment to guide my giving heart.
- My giving heart is pure.
- I don't complain about giving.
- I give to the Lord all the glory due to him as I give to others.
- I've been saved by grace and live my life filled with the Holy Spirit, which is a free gift from my giving, heavenly Father (Ephesians 2:8).
- God gives me so much to give.
- I can never give too much when it's for God.

50

I AM KIND

"The mountains shall depart and the hills be removed, but My kindness shall not depart from you, nor shall My covenant of peace be removed," says the LORD, who has mercy on you.

ISAIAH 54:10

Be kind to one another, tenderhearted, forgiving one another, even as God in Christ forgave you.

EPHESIANS 4:32

Meditate

God tells us to be kind because he is kind. The Lord is good to every human being. We can be numb to this ineffable fact by thinking people have to deserve our kindness. The kindness of God is everywhere you look. It's his kindness that delivers us from evil and protects us from harm. It's his kindness that heals us, gives us courage, and saves us from troubles. It's his kindness that sustains all life.

Jesus was kind in all he was and did while on earth. We might attribute his explosive behavior when he turned over the tables of the money changers in the temple to anger (Matthew 21:12), but it was an act of kindness for God's children who were overcharged for animals they were required to sacrifice. It was not only righteous indignation that drove him but also his kindness. He cared about the poor who were being exploited. His love for the Father and for his children wielded the stick that day, sending the pigeons and ill-gained coins scattering.

Jesus was kind to everyone. On the night Jesus was betrayed, Judas brought a multitude of soldiers with chains and clubs to arrest Jesus, and they were especially cruel. Peter jumped up to defend Jesus and chopped off the right ear of the servant of the high priest. Jesus graciously said, "Permit even this," and calmly reached over, touched the man's head, and healed him (Luke 22:51). You'd think Judas and the great army of armed soldiers would have been stunned by the miracle, but it went right over their heads.

We have a million daily opportunities to express the kindness of God because his kindness lives in us. Making a conscious choice to show kindness can change the very atmosphere and open closed hearts to God's love.

Affirmations

- The kindness of God lives in me.
- I am kind even when I don't feel like it.
- I am kind to others even when they don't show kindness to me.
- I am kind to those who disagree with me.
- I am kind to those who dislike me.
- I am kind to those who don't believe as I do.
- I am kind to myself.
- I ask God to guide the kindness in my heart to take me to the places that need to experience kindness.
- I am committed to kindness in my home.

51

I'M A GOOD LISTENER

"He who has ears to hear, let him hear!"
MATTHEW 11:15

Meditate

There are two kinds of listening. The first is hearing from God and listening for his still, small voice within you. The second is listening and paying attention to the here and now, which is what this meditation will focus on.

Paying attention is one of the greatest skills in life. To observe is to take note or detect. To pay attention is seeing, hearing, and reacting with intention to what you've observed. You can observe or notice something when you're bored or disinterested, but you don't pay attention when you're bored or disinterested, sleeping or daydreaming.

Listening is a skill you can teach yourself. It takes intention to listen when someone goes on a lengthy tirade about something you don't really care about. It's in these moments when something important comes your way and you miss it because you stopped listening.

Boredom is the wicked stepsister to paying attention.[10] It's not easy to listen when you're bored, but the good news is you can develop the skill of being a good listener. It begins with intention, saying the affirmation that you are already a good listener. Friends like talking to you because you listen. Teachers like you in class because

---

10 For more information on boredom, see Meditation 86 titled "Never Bored."

you listen. This skill comes from making the intention to listen, and then quieting your own voice to make space for something someone else is saying.

If you find yourself in an argument with someone and you don't know how to handle it, you'll have to pull out the surprise weapon. There's nothing stronger than this defense skill guaranteed to overcome anything: listen.

Consider the story of a woman who was such a good listener that when she took walks in the woods, even the trees leaned forward to tell her their stories.

Listening to God's still, small voice in you is the best habit to acquire. The second is to encourage others with your nonjudgmental way of listening and caring.

Affirmations

- I am an encouragement to people through my nonjudgmental way of listening and caring.
- When someone starts an argument, I don't lose control and argue. I listen.
- I enjoy hearing what others have to say.
- I listen without interrupting.
- People are drawn to me because I listen when they talk to me.
- When someone disagrees with me, I listen to what they have to say.
- Listening helps me learn and understand new things.
- Knowing how to listen makes me a wiser person.

52

MY FREE TIME

To everything there is a season, a time for every purpose under heaven: a time to be born, and a time to die; a time to plant, and a time to pluck what is planted; a time to kill, and a time to heal; a time to break down, and a time to build up.

ECCLESIASTES 3:1–3

Meditate

What you do in your free time might say more about you than what you do at other times. Whether you have hobbies, train for marathons, read, write, watch TV, or shop, your free time speaks volumes about you. Our free time offers us opportunities to enrich our lives beyond the work we do, so it's as important as other times of our day. If you spend your free time running errands, it's not your free time but your obligation time.

Sometimes we use our free time to simply rest because of a demanding schedule, and this rest is wonderful. Grocery shopping, folding laundry, housekeeping, getting the car detailed, or fixing a leak are not activities we'd call free-time activities or rest. They come under the category of obligation.

When I was in graduate school, I worked a job and served as a psychotherapist intern while raising a family. I had to be creative and let unimportant things go to spend time with my children every day. If you have a family, think about using your free time to have fun together.

Think of your free time as sacred. Your free time should feel invigorating and restorative and should enrich and bless the hours of your day. If your free time isn't enriching, take a few moments now to itemize your daily activities to include what you do in your free time. Ask yourself where God is in your free time. Invite him to share your free time with you.

There's a time to work and a time to play, a time to wash the car and a time to take the kids to the park, a time to fix the garage door and a time to read the Psalms. I will not allow my free time to spend me.

Time with God is separate from the other times of your day. Of course you pray and talk to God during the day, but God time is a separate, private engagement. The more time you give to the Lord, the more your time will seem to multiply. Telling yourself you have no time for God is like saying you have no time for life. Give careful thought to your free time. Use the following affirmations to help you.

Affirmations

- I am wise about how I use my free time, no matter how limited it is.
- I ask God how he would like me to spend my free time.
- I invite God to spend my free time with me.
- I use my free time wisely to enrich my life.

53

DECISIONS

Multitudes, multitudes in the valley of decision!
For the day of the LORD is near in the valley of decision.
JOEL 3:14

Meditate

When I need to make a decision, I know where to go for
help. Sometimes the answers aren't clear to me immediately,
but wisdom and instruction wait for me. No matter how
big my quandary is, I have within me the patience and
resolve to wait. God is in the process of guiding me to make
the decision. He reveals his thoughts to me and shows me
the answers I need (Proverbs 1:23). I use discretion when
making decisions. Some decisions I must make quickly.
Other decisions take a while, and I don't rush them or allow
myself to be anxious because I know God is at work for me.

Everything we do is the result of decision-making.
We make decisions to love and to hate, to judge, or to show
compassion. Forgiveness is a decision. There's a significant
process of forgiveness among the Babemba tribe in South
Africa.

> When a person acts irresponsibly or unjustly, he
> is placed in the center of the village, alone and
> unfettered. All work ceases, and every man, woman,
> and child in the village gathers in a large circle
> around the accused individual. Then each person in
> the tribe speaks to the accused, one at a time, each

recalling the good things the person in the center of the circle has done in his lifetime. Every incident, every experience that can be recalled with any detail and accuracy, is recounted. All his positive attributes, good deeds, strengths, and kindnesses are recited carefully and at length. This tribal ceremony often lasts for several days. At the end, the tribal circle is broken, a joyous celebration takes place, and the person is symbolically and literally welcomed back into the tribe.[11]

This passage shows an entire village making the same decision to forgive and restore. Imagine an entire community, city, or family making a joint decision to forgive. All the goodness we do is the result of decisions we've made. All the evil we do, as well, is the result of decisions we make.

Affirmations

- Today I affirm and proclaim that I will not make decisions in haste.
- I am very careful about the decisions I make that could hurt others.
- I reject all self-centered decision-making.
- I reject and renounce decisions made in anger.
- I reject and renounce decisions made in fear.
- I reject and renounce the decision not to forgive.

---

11 Jack Kornfield, *The Art of Forgiveness, Lovingkindness, and Peace* (New York: Bantam Dell, 2008), 42.

54

MY BODY

God said, "Let us make humankind in our image,
after our likeness."
GENESIS 1:26 NET

When He had given thanks, He broke it and said,
"Take, eat; this is My body which is broken for you;
do this in remembrance of Me."
1 CORINTHIANS 11:24

Do you not know that your body is the temple of the Holy
Spirit who is in you, whom you have from God, and you
are not your own? For you were bought at a price; therefore
glorify God in your body.
1 CORINTHIANS 6:19–20

Meditate

When the Lord Jesus lived on this earth, he lived in a
human body, same as you and I live in human bodies.
While still a young man, he sacrificed his body to a
tortuous death not only for our souls but also for our
bodies. How do we honor the body Jesus lived in and died
in for us? By honoring ours. As a counselor, I work with
men and women who disregard the holiness of their bodies.
Not you, I hope. You fully comprehend that your body is
a temple for the Holy Spirit to reside in, just like the Holy
Spirit dwelled in Jesus.

We all know our bodies need food to nourish them
and keep them in working order. We exercise to keep them

strong, clothe them, and house them. The important factor in caring for our bodies is to remember that, as temples of the Holy Spirit, our bodies are holy real estate. From brushing our teeth to eating our greens and getting six to eight hours of sleep a night, it's imperative we be familiar with our body's needs and temperaments. (Your body can get moody too.) Holy temples require maintenance, repair, constant care, and much respect.

Honor and love your body. Bless each part. Be awed at the mystery of it. Honor your body because the relationship you have with your body is lifelong, and it's not going anywhere without you.

Affirmations

- My body takes working orders from me, so I treat it with care.
- I thank God for my body, which is so good to me.
- I honor my body and stop putting it down and finding fault with it.
- I honor my body and stop complaining about it.
- When my body is in the valley of illness, I pray for healing and speak gentle healing words to it, and God heals me (1 Peter 2:24; Psalm 103:4).
- I am not obsessed with my body. My body does not rule over my life.
- I am so blessed to have the body God has given me.

55

SLEEP

When you lie down, you will not be afraid;
yes, you will lie down and your sleep will be sweet.
PROVERBS 3:24

I will both lie down in peace, and sleep;
for You alone, O LORD, make me dwell in safety.
PSALM 4:8

Meditate

I've worked with many Christians who have sleep problems.
We all have sleepless nights now and then, and it's good to
know what to do about it. Most of the time our emotional
state keeps us awake. Other times our minds are frantically
at work, and we have a daily planner in which we're
mentally scribbling away all during the night.

God loves to give us sweet sleep. He holds us in his
arms of peace every time we climb into our beds. If you
feel agitated at bedtime, you'll take the agitation to bed
with you. If you fail to drop the activities of the day before
you go to bed, you'll go on living them. The peace of God
doesn't reach you; you're too busy living your daytime at
night. Being tired doesn't guarantee a peaceful sleep, and
exhaustion can make you restless. Your brain needs rest
as well as your body. I have spoken of the skills of stillness
and inner peace throughout this book. Bedtime is time to
practice what you've learned.

At bedtime, put your awake self aside. Make room for your sleep. Here are some affirmations to speak to yourself at bedtime. Speak the affirmations slowly, allowing them to quietly draw you into the presence of God and rest. Continue to gently affirm Scripture verses to yourself and give the words space to go deep inside as they make a permanent nighttime home in you. Give your pillow a hug with Proverbs 3:24: "You will lie down and your sleep will be sweet."

Affirmations

- I quiet my waking hours to make room for my sleep hours.
- I lay aside every activity of the day so I can enter my quiet sleep time.
- I quiet my mind and set aside busy thoughts for tomorrow.
- I have nowhere to go, nothing to do, and nothing to think about as I climb into my bed.
- At bedtime, I surrender every muscle of my body to relax in the peace of God.
- I surrender every memory, plan, idea, opinion, worry, goal, and musing now for a sweet and peaceful sleep.
- Angels watch over me.
- The sweetness of sleep embraces me as the Holy Spirit gently guides my mind to sleep.
- When I lie down, my sleep is sweet.

56

GRACE

"My grace is sufficient for you."
2 CORINTHIANS 12:9

Meditate

The best way to understand God's grace is to think of it as favor we haven't earned. Grace is God paying attention and giving us his unearned approval and support. The word *grace* comes from the Greek word *charis*, which means "favor." It's mentioned 150 times in the New Testament. Unmerited favor is what we inherited when we said yes to Jesus and were spiritually born again. It's by the grace of God that we're a part of his family by no merit of our own. Unmerited favor continues to live in us as we live our lives in Christ. His grace pulls us up from the futility of self-sufficiency.

Grace differs from mercy. Both grace and mercy are grounded in love. However, the Greek word for "mercy" is *eleos*, which means "pity." Grace is a free gift of God and includes every blessing of God. Mercy infers forgiveness and compassion, which lead to a walk in grace. When we walk in grace, we walk in favor and blessings. Favor is exalting. Favor raises us up, bringing a multitude of blessings. We need to honor God's gift of grace. It doesn't give us freedom to do whatever we want. Jesus promises never to leave us alone, but when we're out of his will, we lose intimacy with him. Life will become dark and shadowy with our egos running the show. Every blessing we experience is born of grace.

Affirmations

- I'm a child of grace.
- I live in God's grace, the fullness of life and the embodiment of love.
- I'm beautiful in God's grace.
- God gives me his favor as a free gift. I can't earn it.
- I honor the grace given to me by God and praise him for counting me worthy of his attention.
- It's by God's grace that I'm a child of God.
- God approves of me.
- God isn't looking for me to impress him.

57

HARMONY

The multitude of them that believed
were of one heart and of one soul.
ACTS 4:32 KJV

Two are better than one, because they have a good
reward for their labor. For if they fall, one will lift up his
companion. But woe to him who is alone when he falls, for
he has no one to help him up.
ECCLESIASTES 4:9–10

Meditate

Harmony among Christians is a reflection of heaven.
Loving one another and caring for each other's needs like
the believers of the early church in the book of Acts is a
beautiful model for us today. Christian brothers and sisters
love, help, grow with, pray for, and enjoy each other. Jesus
was implicit when he commanded us to love one another:
"This is my commandment, that you love one another as I
have loved you" (John 13:34, author's paraphrase). He said
it more than once; that's how important it was to him.

It's not possible to love one another if we don't live in
harmony, and it's not possible to live in harmony if we don't
love one another.

Churches are thriving today in all corners of the
world, and we're all different. There are roughly forty
thousand denominations globally with different modes
of worship. It doesn't mean we're divided; it means we're

different. There are different cultures, environments, ages, languages, classes, modes of music, and leadership, but our faith and doctrine are rock solid in Christ Jesus and the Gospels (Acts 9:31). Not all churches are Christian, of course, and Paul admonishes us to be spiritually aware of false teachers and false prophets (2 Peter 2:1). Our harmony among Christian believers must be strictly centered on Jesus Christ, who died on the cross, was resurrected from the dead, and reigns supreme over the globe now.

We're called family, and our family extends around the globe. Jesus said in John 13:35 that our love for one another would be seen by all. That's the promise that harmony holds out to us. "That He might present [us] to Himself a glorious church [us], not having spot or wrinkle or any such thing, but that she should be holy and without blemish" (Ephesians 5:27).

Affirmations

- I am a peacemaker.
- I do not judge or find fault with my Christian brothers and sisters.
- I do not discriminate.
- My love for my Christian brothers and sisters is nonnegotiable and permanently engraved in me with the seal of John 3:16.
- I am a Christian who puts God's loving-kindness first.
- I am God's agent of harmony.

58

HELPING PEOPLE

Whenever we have an opportunity,
let us do good to all people,
and especially to those who belong to the family of faith.
GALATIANS 6:10 NET

Pay careful attention to all these things I am commanding
you so that it may always go well with you and your
children after you when you do what is good and right in
the sight of the LORD your God.
DEUTERONOMY 12:28 NET

Meditate

Be prepared to help someone at the drop of a hat. Don't
even think twice when it's in your power to do something
good for someone. You could be saving someone's life.
When my children and I moved to California from
Minnesota, I was new to ocean swimming and knew
nothing about riptides and their deadly turbulence. I went
for a swim and became caught in the torrent of the riptide,
which is like being a punching bag for the raging current,
and was hurtled like seaweed through the water. Being
tossed about so violently, I didn't know which end was up,
and I lost all sense of direction. I lost my breath and gulped
water, and at one point, I threw myself to the surface,
and for a split second, I saw a beautiful sight. A man was
swimming toward me to help. I was tossed again, but I
managed another glimpse at the surface a few seconds later,

and I saw the man turn around and swim in the opposite direction back to shore. I'll never forget that sight. There's nothing to compare it to. Someone was coming to save me from drowning, and then he turned back.

This is the image I carry when something looks too hard for me to do for someone or when I don't want to do something. I remember drowning and watching help swim away. Fortunately, a lifeguard looking through his binoculars from his tower down the beach saw me struggling in the riptide and rescued me using a boat.

As children of God, it's important to keep our spiritual eyes and ears open for anyone in need, no matter who or where or what they're into. No one is ever helpless in this world when God sends someone to help.

Affirmations

- I keep my heart open for the needs of others.
- I am wise when helping others to be sure it's God calling me to them.
- I honor those who try to help me but can't.
- I love serving God by helping others.
- I love to help and bless others in any way that they need.
- I am blessed when I bless others with my help.
- My motive for helping others is empathy, not pity. When I pity someone, I make myself the hero, but when I am empathetic, I make us brothers and sisters.

59

TO HAVE EMPATHY

"He must become greater;
I must become less."
JOHN 3:30 NIV

"I have been crucified with Christ; it is no longer I who live,
but Christ lives in me; and the life which I now live in the
flesh I live by faith in the Son of God, who loved me and
gave Himself for me."
GALATIANS 2:20

Be imitators of me, as I am of Christ.
1 CORINTHIANS 11:1 ESV

Meditate

Empathy is the ability to feel what another person feels,
put yourself in their shoes, really understand, and know
the other person's feelings. Empathy can help you avoid an
argument by understanding the other person's perspective,
if only for a minute.

Empathy is a close relative to love and caring; all
are compassionate and kind. But just because you love or
care for someone doesn't mean you're always empathic
toward them. In marriages the partners may love each
other, but they may not be able to really know the other's
feelings by putting themselves in their shoes. Likewise, if
you're trying to help someone and you lack empathy, you
won't know what they're feeling or what they really want or
need. Genuine love includes empathy, and those feelings

of tenderness that accompany empathy can allow us to understand others and care more deeply for their needs.

The Holy Spirit gives Christians the ability to understand others' emotions and feelings, both positive and negative. When we consider the other person's feelings and experiences, we're in the best position to help them. We feel *empathy* for that person. You, as a child of God, are naturally open to the Lord's leading. Allow the Holy Spirit to show you ways to help someone by being empathetic.

Understanding the feelings of another person is a gift most of us were born with, but the lives we've lived inform our levels of empathy. We can always grow more empathetic. If you want to function with compassion, follow Paul's admonition to be an imitator of Christ (1 Corinthians 11:1). Think like Jesus thinks. He feels everything we feel (1 Corinthians 2:16).

Affirmations

- I am aware of what it means to have empathy for someone.
- I open my heart to understand another's feelings when we don't agree.
- I choose empathy over an argument.
- I put myself in another's shoes to experience what they're feeling.
- I don't always have to be right.

60

EXPECTATIONS

In all your ways submit to him,
and he will make your paths straight.
PROVERBS 3:6 NIV

Meditate

Much of our suffering comes from having unrealistic expectations. We expect something or someone outside us to satisfy our needs and wants. We make demands for life to be what it cannot be. It's like believing the advertisements lighting up billboards that shout, "You need this!" The billboards offer us nothing. Advertisements aren't information. I keep telling you in these meditations to know yourself as God knows you, to see yourself as God sees you. When you do this, you'll see what's influencing you and your expectations. It's time to live free from the false ideas of what life owes you.

When our expectations are one with God's, we're able to release our worldly, egotistical expectations that birth nothing but pain. If you're greatly influenced by the beguiling popular culture around you, you'll think like popular culture. Your expectations will be tainted by false thinking. Expectations aren't the same as hope in that expectations are more like demands. Hope looks toward the future but isn't necessarily demanding. Examine your expectations. Recognize the false from the true. Many of your expectations of others, especially loved ones, make demands. Even your expectations of God can be more like demands. The Bible doesn't tell us to make demands of God. It tells us to pray and believe.

Choose godly, positive expectations. Your positive expectations affirm and expect the will of the Lord to be done on earth as in heaven. When you affirm the truth, you can expect the truth. Psalm 55:22 says to cast our burdens on the Lord, and that includes our expectations. Make the following affirmations your lifestyle. The love you give is without contingencies like "I'll love you *if*—" Take a look at the list of the fruit of the Holy Spirit (Galatians 5:22–26). Live in them and give them to the world.

God expects your expectations to be positive and aligned with his. Expect blessings, love, goodness, health, wholeness, and every benefit of the kingdom of God. You'll live in the great expectation of God's fulfilled promises.

Affirmations

- I release the unmet expectations I have of the world around me.
- I expect love, joy, and peace to flow continuously from me.
- I do not harbor silent expectations for other people to meet.
- I don't allow myself to be abused because of my false expectations.
- I do not expect the world to make me happy.
- The world owes me nothing. God gives me everything.

61

ENDURANCE

You have need of endurance, so that after you have
done the will of God, you may receive the promise.
HEBREWS 10:36

Therefore we also, since we are surrounded by so great a
cloud of witnesses, let us lay aside every weight, and the sin
which so easily ensnares us, and let us run with endurance
the race that is set before us.
HEBREWS 12:1

Meditate

I give you the following example of extreme endurance for
you to compare to the endurance required of you now in
your present situation.

Here's how the runners I know train for a hundred-
mile race (yes, there is such a thing): they need both
discipline and endurance. Discipline is needed to get up
early and maintain the routine, but it's endurance that
gives them the stamina to keep going day after day, week
after week, month after month. The hundred-mile race
takes six to nine months of training, which includes two
consecutive races of thirty-one to sixty-two miles per
week. The hundred-mile race includes nonstop running for
twenty-eight to thirty hours while carrying supplies like
a waterproof jacket, spare warm clothes, food, and drink.
Runners say they're in pain most of the time and feel sick
along the way too. There's also the danger of tripping on

tree roots and getting stuck in mud and navigating hilly terrain. It's endurance that runners desperately need in order to stay focused.

You and I may not be training for a hundred-mile race, but we need the same kind of endurance for our personal race of life. Endurance takes pacing. Start slowly and stick to the plan. When you finally arrive at the finish line, endurance takes a bow. Endurance is like a best friend: you couldn't have finished the race without it.

Faith also takes endurance. Without endurance, faith is weak and on the flimsy side. Just like it takes commitment to run a race, faith requires commitment to endure life's hurdles. Don't permit temptation, rejection, physical pain, emotional pain, or other obstacles to soil or deter your faith. No matter how arduous, you're on the track heading for the finish line.

A great celebration waits for you there.

Affirmations

- I can endure anything. I am a person of faith.
- Within me is supernatural endurance to keep me strong and on course.
- I will endure anything necessary to fulfill a task set before me by the Lord.
- One day I will say with Paul, "I have fought the good fight, I have finished the race, I have kept the faith" (2 Timothy 4:7).

62

HOW'S YOUR DAY GOING?

Kind words are like honey.
PROVERBS 16:24 NLT

Meditate

How's your day going? That's a familiar question, isn't it? Everyone says it. Clerks in stores, restaurant servers when taking your order, voices on the telephone as you wait for your bank statement, friends at home, your spouse. Not a week goes by without someone asking how your day is going. It's a friendly gesture.

Once, just as a little experiment, when a clerk at a cash register asked me that familiar question, I whined back, "My dog died, my cat has distemper, and I have to have foot surgery." I added, "And this is just in one day."

The young man shot me a blank look and, handing me my receipt, said, "Have a nice day."

We both proved something with our exchange that day: we don't really care how anyone's day is going.

When God asks, *How is your day going?* he's not just making small talk. We could translate "Where are you, Adam?" in the garden after he ate the forbidden fruit to "How is your day going?" Of course God knew how Adam's day was going, and he knows how your day is going. He wants you to talk about it, to go into it with him.

Hagar was dying of thirst in the desert with her son, Ishmael, after being expelled from her home with Abraham and Sarah. "What's wrong, Hagar?" God asked. There she was, desperate and half-dead, and God sent an angel to ask if anything was wrong. Of course God knew exactly what was wrong, and he provided a miraculous well of water for her and the boy to drink from and encouraged her to continue the journey.

When God asks you, *How is your day going?* it's not the same as a person asking it. He knows the answer, but he wants to hear it from you. He will ask how your day is going if you're drunk in a bar or praying in church. Sometimes the question will startle you, wake you up, convict you, or thrill you.

When we answer God truthfully, we get a good look at ourselves. God, who knows everything, wants to hear it from us. Be real. Be honest. He can handle both agony and ecstasy.

Affirmations

- I do not take the moments of my day for granted.
- I can connect with God openly and honestly.
- My day goes well when I am fully aware of the presence of God wherever I am and whatever I'm doing.
- My life is God's.
- Love calls me to God, and love calls God to me.
- I am secure in God's watching over me and caring for every aspect of my daily life.
- I love to tell the Lord how my day is going because he cares more than any person.

63

WORRY

"Take my yoke upon you. Let me teach you,
because I am humble and gentle at heart,
and you will find rest for your souls."
MATTHEW 11:29 NLT

One thing I do, forgetting those things which are behind
and reaching forward to those things which are ahead.
PHILIPPIANS 3:13

Meditate

Worry is a subtle disease. It creeps up in you, and you
don't even know it's been fermenting in you for perhaps
your whole life. As children we all worried. We had a lot
to worry about, surrounded by such a big world we had
no control over. *What's going to happen to me? Why is this
happening? What if I lose something or someone? What
about me?*

We're still worrying about the same things as adults.
Worry is 100 percent connected to fear. I was a firstborn
child, and my father's work took him out of town for weeks
at a time. This left my mother alone with her newborn baby
without a break. I was with her day and night. As I grew
into a toddler, I was so attached to my mother I couldn't
handle being away from her for any amount of time. She
took me everywhere with her, and if she were to leave to
go shopping without me, I would panic uncontrollably.
She took my world with her. My attachment to her lasted

until she died, but as I matured, my need for her turned to respect. I honored and appreciated her with all my heart. As an adult, I've had to renounce the worries and fears I developed as a child. It's important to recognize that worry can open the door to demonic oppression and that we must quickly renounce it in Jesus' name.

We think worry is normal, but worry thwarts our faith, ruins our health, and seriously wounds our souls. On the bright side, conquering and renouncing worry opens the door to a more dynamic, spirit-filled life in Christ. The rehabilitated, delivered worrier is a world changer and helps restore the lives of other worriers.

Christians can also experience the disease of worry. I have worked with people in counseling who worry about everything from God hurling his fury and wrath on the world to being doomed to hell for committing the unpardonable sin. If this is you, I suggest rereading the affirmations on endurance and visualization in this book. It's time we rise up and take our place in God's great army of healthy spirits and souls, banning worry from our sanctified doorsteps.

Affirmations

- I renounce worry from my life right now.
- I affirm this day the benefits God has for me in Psalm 103:1–5.
- I am a new person in Christ, and I am healed from the disease of worry.
- I replace worry with the mighty gift of faith.

64

LOVE YOUR ENEMIES

"You have heard that it was said, 'You shall love your neighbor and hate your enemy.' But I say to you, love your enemies, bless those who curse you, do good to those who hate you, and pray for those who spitefully use you and persecute you, that you may be sons of your Father in heaven; for He makes His sun rise on the evil and on the good, and sends rain on the just and on the unjust."

MATTHEW 5:43–45

"Be merciful, just as your Father also is merciful."
LUKE 6:36

Meditate

There's no commandment of Jesus quite as befuddling as the commandment to love our enemies.

It's not possible to love our enemies the same way we love the people close to us, of course, but what kind of love is Jesus talking about then? To love our enemies as Jesus commands us means that no matter what a person does or people do to us by abusing, insulting, or injuring us, we ask for nothing for them but their highest good.

Love for loved ones comes easily. It's not hard to love friends, spouses, children, and people who are loving and caring toward us. But to want the best for our enemies is a stretch. It takes spiritual stretching most of us aren't accustomed to. But this love toward our enemies is vital to our peace of mind.

Jesus' commandment to love our enemies brings out two great points. First, he takes our attention off revenge, hatred, bitterness, and all the responses that we experience when we're wronged or wounded. Second, by loving our enemies and by praying for the best for them, like Jesus himself did, we become free.

God sends his rain on the just and the unjust (Matthew 5:45). He is kind to the man or woman who brings him joy and equally kind to the man or woman who grieves his heart. God's love embraces saints and sinners alike. It's that love we marvel at and praise him for. We live and thrive in the almighty, loving embrace of perfect, unchanging, and transforming love.

Affirmations

- Jesus commanded me to pray for the best for my enemies, and I obey.
- I do not harbor bitterness and anger toward those who hurt, despise, or bully me.
- In the name of Jesus, I show God's mercy on sinner and saint alike.
- I am not revengeful.
- God has opened my eyes to look deeper into his nature, and I choose to be like him.
- I pray for my enemies' highest good.

65

MYSTERIES OF GOD

He [Jesus] answered and said to them,
"Because it has been given to you to know
the mysteries of the kingdom of heaven."
MATTHEW 13:11

Let a man so consider us, as servants of Christ
and stewards of the mysteries of God.
1 CORINTHIANS 4:1

Meditate

Mysteries of the kingdom are those truths that have been hidden from past ages. What are those mysteries? All the mysteries of the past generations are wrapped up in one man: Jesus Christ. Love for Jesus is the starting point for understanding the hidden mysteries of wisdom and knowledge. Love is not an intellectual endeavor. You can't understand God with your mind. That's why his ways are a mystery to the natural mind. God's love for you and your love for God are the root of everything you know. You live to know God. The mysteries of God, according to the Bible, are never revealed by opinion, conjecture, or looking anywhere other than his Word for spiritual enlightenment and understanding. Romans 1:25 makes this eminently clear: "They traded the truth about God for a lie. So they worshiped and served the things God created instead of the Creator himself, who is worthy of eternal praise!" (NLT).

The church is referred to as a mystery in the Word (Ephesians 5:32), and Paul asked the church for prayer to be able to boldly speak the mysterious plan of the good news of God (6:19).

Jesus clearly affirms in Matthew 13:11 that the ability to comprehend spiritual truth is graciously given by God to his chosen ones, those who are filled with his Holy Spirit and love his beloved only begotten Son, Jesus.

Affirmations

- The Holy Spirit reveals the mysteries of the kingdom of God.
- I can't understand the kingdom of God without the Holy Spirit.
- I find the mysteries of the kingdom of God thrilling as I continue daily to study and pray the Scriptures.
- Jesus hears my prayers for wisdom and understanding regarding the mysteries of God.
- God's will is not a mystery to me but a revelation.

66

I AM FILLED WITH WISDOM

If anyone is deficient in wisdom, he should ask God,
who gives to all generously and without reprimand,
and it will be given to him.

JAMES 1:5 NET

Who is wise and understanding among you?
By his good conduct let him show his works
in the meekness of wisdom.

JAMES 3:13 ESV

Meditate

When we make decisions too quickly and things go all
wrong, we say things like, "That was stupid" or "How could
I be so dumb?" You're not stupid, and you're not dumb.
You may have missed the mark with the decision, but that
does not mean you are dumb or stupid. Often, we make
decisions too soon without waiting for the guidance of
the Holy Spirit. When we're upset, angry, or impatient,
we often say and do things we regret later if we don't wait
for wisdom. Anger leads to acting impetuously and never
generates wisdom.

Wisdom, an attribute and gift of the Holy Spirit,
lives in you and is ready to be put into action. Wisdom
doesn't just show up out of the blue without advance notice
and some prior work on your part. God will increase his
wisdom in you when you ask, but the secret is to make
thinking and acting in wisdom your lifestyle. This takes

practice. Study the Proverbs and memorize the words of Jesus. Call on wisdom before jumping into your own resources for guidance.

Wisdom is power, and it's important for you to give serious attention to two vital points: (1) What is wisdom? Describe it to yourself. What does the fruit of wisdom bring? What are wisdom's long-lasting effects? (2) What is the One giving you wisdom like? How does he think and act? Don't confuse wisdom with cleverness. God's wisdom is consistent and permanent with the stability of heaven, but human cleverness is fickle and erases itself with change and time.

Wisdom and meekness were one in Jesus (James 3:13). The Greek word for "meekness" here is *prautes*, and it means "gentleness." Wisdom is gentle and like God because Jesus is both gentle and wise (Matthew 11:29). Wisdom is power. His gentle power of wisdom is yours.

Affirmations

- I am wise.
- I practice wisdom as a lifestyle.
- I make myself open and ready to receive wisdom from God each time I ask.
- I work at being wise by quieting down and waiting for guidance from the Lord.
- I am growing in God's wisdom every day.
- I am filled with the gentle power of wisdom.
- My wisdom is a blessing to others.

67

I CHOOSE MY FRIENDS CAREFULLY

Do you not know that friendship
with the world is enmity with God?
JAMES 4:4

A man who has friends must himself be friendly,
but there is a friend who sticks closer than a brother.
PROVERBS 18:24

Meditate

A friend who sticks closer than a brother is something
rare in the selfish culture of today. Usually that kind of
friendship is built over a number of years. People living in
small communities tend to be closer than those in large
cities. Megachurches depend on small home groups to
create close friendships among the believers. As Christians,
our best friends will be those who share our faith, and
that's because every relationship has a spiritual component
to it. The Bible warns us against giving our allegiance in
friendship to those who have no respect or deep interest
in God. It's tempting to adapt to a worldly lifestyle, leaving
God out just to have friends.

Sometimes we don't choose friends carefully because
of our need for friends, any friends. Having a friendship
is more than sharing likes and interests like people do on
dating sites. The child of God looks into the heart of a
friend to see what's there to love and honor, to see God.

Choose friends who nourish and inspire you to be all you can be in the Lord. Choose friends whom you can respect and who will respect you. One mark of a true friend is one you can be quiet with, a friend with whom you're both comfortable just being in the same room.

Affirmations

- I am grateful I have friends who love God.
- I am blessed to be the friend who sticks closer than a brother (or sister).
- I am a good and faithful friend.
- I love to pray and share the Lord with my friends.
- Not everyone is a friend, not even family.
- I do not judge my friends.
- I do not accept judging and faultfinding in my relationships.
- A friend who continually finds fault is not a friend.
- I am a friend of God.
- I cherish friends with whom I can share silence in the presence of God.

68

ENCOURAGING

Arise, go out and speak kindly and encouragingly.
2 SAMUEL 19:7 AMPC

Hezekiah spoke encouragingly to all the Levites who had
good understanding in the Lord's work. So the people ate
the seven-day appointed feast, offering peace offerings,
making confession [and giving thanks] to the Lord, the
God of their fathers.
2 CHRONICLES 30:22 AMPC

Anxiety in a man's heart weighs it down,
but an encouraging word makes it glad.
PROVERBS 12:25 AMPC

Meditate

No matter how down I get, an encouraging word has the
power to change everything. Encouragement exists all
throughout the Bible from Genesis to Revelation. Scripture
is our greatest encouragement, a demonstration of the
love God gives his children. We have the power to change
lives with our encouragement. It's also in our power to
encourage ourselves. The affirmations that follow are to
affirm the continuous encouragement of the Lord and his
extreme loving concern for everything in your life. You
live in the arms of the Lord's leading. He's encouraging
you through every minute of every day, twenty-four seven.
Therefore, you can give the same loving encouragement to
others, and that honors God.

Affirmations

- I have the inner power of the Holy Spirit to lift myself up through the Word of God, my holy and perfect encouragement.

- The name of the Lord is a strong tower, and I encourage myself and others to run to it for eternal safety, warmth, and love (Proverbs 18:10).

- I will not permit the condition of the world to bring me to despair as though I'm not a child of God and don't have a home under the shadow of the Almighty (Psalm 91:1).

- I study and absorb God's Word into my heart and soul to always stay encouraged.

- I'm encouraged to be steadfast and immovable in my faith (1 Corinthians 15:58).

- I put a stop to feeling sorry for myself.

- I am encouraged by the words of Jesus when he said the work of the Lord is to believe in him (John 6:29).

- My faith and holy trust in Jesus grow daily.

69

DISCERNMENT

"When he, the Spirit of truth, comes,
he will guide you into all the truth."
JOHN 16:13 NIV

Solid food is for the mature, who by constant use have
trained themselves to distinguish good from evil.
HEBREWS 5:14 NIV

Meditate

The gift of discernment, or the gift of the discerning of
spirits, is not a judging spirit. Discernment has no opinion.
It's a gift of recognizing something that's not available to
the natural senses. Hebrews 5:14 explains that discernment
is a spiritual gift for the mature Christian to distinguish
good from evil. Discernment differentiates between true
and false. It distinguishes the work of God from the work of
darkness (1 John 4:1). It's one of the nine gifts of the Holy
Spirit found in 1 Corinthians 12.

      Spiritual discernment is not to be confused with
perception or intuition in the natural realm; instead, it's
an inner knowing given by God. People use their gift of
discernment to help them see through a lie, to recognize
bad intentions toward their child, or to perceive danger
when, outwardly, things look fine. Discernment is a
powerful and crucial gift for spiritual awareness and
protection.

The Holy Spirit's gift of discernment is not the same as suspicion. Suspicion might lead to false accusation, and this can be a serious mistake. Be very wary of feelings of suspicion. Before you act on them, pray for wisdom and discernment and wait on God for spiritual clarity. Religious suspicion among Puritans in America led to the New England witch hunts of 1638–1725, in which over three hundred women were accused of witchcraft.[12] The allegations were baseless.

The Holy Spirit's gift of discernment is always available to you. It can be a feeling and a certain sense, a holy awareness. Your gift of discernment is a protection and help for making decisions.

Affirmations

- I operate with the gift of discernment.
- I recognize the work of God.
- I lead a spirit-filled life (Ephesians 5:18).
- I do not make a judgment and call it Holy Spirit discernment.
- I do not act with suspicion and call it Holy Spirit discernment.
- I constantly practice my gift of discernment to distinguish good from evil.
- The Holy Spirit's discernment protects and makes me aware of what is true and what is false.

12 Bridget Marshall, "Most Witches Are Women, Because Witch Hunts Were All about Persecuting the Powerless," The Conversation, October 23, 2019, https://theconversation.com/most-witches-are-women-because-witch-hunts-were-all-about-persecuting-the-powerless-125427.

70

DELIVERANCE

"He has sent me to heal the brokenhearted,
to preach deliverance to the captives."
LUKE 4:16–19 PHILLIPS

Look, the LORD's hand is not too weak to deliver you;
his ear is not too deaf to hear you.
ISAIAH 59:1 NET

Meditate

The word *deliver* appears 383 times throughout the Bible. *To deliver* means to take someone from one place and release them into another. *Deliverance* means the state of being set free or the state of being rescued. God delivered the Israelites out of bondage, and he'll do the same for us.

Joseph's story in Genesis is a good example of deliverance. Joseph's brothers did a terrible, ungodly thing when they sold him into slavery. Years later, when Joseph had earned the title of second-in-command to Pharaoh, his brothers showed up in Egypt to beg Pharaoh for food because of a famine in Israel. The shock must have been dreadful when they realized it was their little brother whom they stood before to beg. Joseph told them that they had meant their act of cruelty for evil, but unknown to them, God used it for good.

Joseph said in Genesis 45:7, "God sent me before you to preserve you a posterity in the earth, and to save your lives by a great *deliverance*" (KJV, emphasis added). Rejoicing is often associated with deliverance.

David wrote in Psalm 34:17, "When the righteous cry for help, the LORD hears and delivers them out of all their troubles" (ESV). God said in Psalm 50:15, "Call upon me in the day of trouble; I will deliver you, and you shall glorify me" (ESV). Our deliverance glorifies God.

Colossians 1:13 tells us, "He has delivered us from the domain of darkness and transferred us to the kingdom of his beloved Son" (ESV).

Affirmations

- I accept the delivering power of the shed blood of Jesus.
- God has delivered me from the pain of the past.
- God has turned bad into good in my life for his glory.
- I am rescued from sin and free to live my life fully and wholly as a child of God.
- I am delivered from the false thinking that has kept me in darkness.
- I am a child of light, for I am delivered from darkness.
- I am rescued from evil.

71

I AM NONJUDGMENTAL

"Why do you see the speck in your brother's eye, but fail to see the beam of wood in your own? How can you say to your brother, 'Brother, let me remove the speck from your eye,' while you yourself don't see the beam in your own? You hypocrite! First remove the beam from your own eye, and then you can see clearly to remove the speck from your brother's eye."

LUKE 6:41–42 NET

Meditate

I recognize the fruitless pressure I put on others to meet my expectations and values, but often I don't meet my own expectations and values. When that happens, I judge myself, which makes me feel guilty and terrible about myself. These are wasted emotions. The closer I stay to Jesus, the clearer it becomes to me that there are no other powers on earth as boundless as compassion and love.

God always calls us to him and never pushes us away with dismissive judging. The Holy Spirit in me guides me to treat myself with respect and to treat others with respect. The words of Jesus show me it's a character wound to be judgmental and to practice faultfinding. The Holy Spirit's work in me always leads to honoring others no matter what I think is wrong with them.

Passing judgment on myself and others is nothing like the Holy Spirit's gentle correction. If I'm falling off track, it's love that draws me back home. Judgment pushes me further away. Correction helps to increase my faith. Condemnation breaks my heart. It's God's love that corrects me and sets me free from sin. Judgment points out my sin and makes me feel guilty and ashamed. Love points out my sin, and I'm humbled and ask for forgiveness. To judge another drives compassion out the door. I open that door when I drop the habit of judging.

Affirmations

- I'm continually aware that we are all important to God.
- I am free from the soul prison of thinking I am more important than others.
- I drop my self-appointed opinions and do not lean on my own feeble, biased understanding.
- The Lord takes my negative thinking, opinions, and feelings and restores my soul's capacity for love. My heart overflows with the compassion of the Lord (Psalm 23:3, 5).
- I no longer find fault and pass judgment on others as that pulls me away from a deeper faith in God.
- The Holy Spirit's work in me always says not to judge no matter what I think is wrong with someone.
- The Holy Spirit reminds me of the wisdom God grants me, and I recall the plank that's stuck in my eye before I try to pull the splinter out of someone else's eye.

72

THE NAME JESUS

These are written that you may believe that Jesus is the Christ, the Son of God, and that believing you may have life in His name.

JOHN 20:31

"Let it be known to you all, and to all the people of Israel, that by the name of Jesus Christ of Nazareth, whom you crucified, whom God raised from the dead, by Him this man stands here before you whole."

ACTS 4:10

Meditate

Jesus told us to pray in his name. To pray in Jesus' name means to pray with holy authority. "In Jesus' name" isn't only a nice tagline to end our prayers but a way to experience the very same access to God that Jesus had when on earth. To pray in Jesus' name means to invoke his standing with our Father.

In prayer we bring our love for others and the world to God in Jesus' name before the throne of grace. Prayer in his name opens God's heart and heaven's resources to hear us and answer us.

Jesus said all authority in heaven and on earth has been given to him (Matthew 28:18). There is no other name on earth with the authority of Jesus' name. The apostles Peter and John understood the authority of the name of Jesus, and the proof of this can be found at the beginning of Acts 3. One day as they walked together to the temple at the hour of prayer, they came upon a beggar sitting at the gate. He was crippled from birth, and someone carried him to the temple gate every day to beg. He saw Peter and John and, with his head down, reached out his hand for alms. Peter told him to raise his head and look at them. The man did, and Peter, with his eyes fixed on his, said, "Silver and gold I do not have, but what I do have I give to you." Then in his next breath he said, "In the name of Jesus Christ of Nazareth, rise up and walk" (v. 6).

That's taking authority. In the name of Jesus, the man's ankles and legs were immediately strengthened, and he leaped to his feet. As the healed man went leaping about and praising God, Peter explained to the amazed crowd that gathered that it was no human being who healed the beggar. Peter gave the man what he had, and that's what we do when we pray. We give what we have: our faith in the name of Jesus Christ of Nazareth.

Affirmations

- I love the name of Jesus.
- I honor the name of Jesus.
- I praise the name of Jesus.
- I pray with the name of Jesus because I love him and want only his will.
- I speak the name of Jesus to remind myself of God's presence and power.

73

GOD'S WORD

"Heaven and earth will pass away,
but my words will never pass away."
MARK 13:31 NIV

Meditate

Here are five reasons why I read the Word of God:

1. *To know God, his character, and his heart.* The first
   thing I learned about God when I was a child is
   that he is love (1 John 4:8). Every passing year,
   I experience more of it. Through his Word, he
   makes himself known for who he is, and I learn
   how to pray, worship, and love him back. I read
   the Word of God to open my heart and mind to
   the Holy Spirit as he teaches me about God.

2. *To build an indestructible foundation for my soul.*
   My soul is renewed, restored, and built strong in
   the Lord as he leads me in the right path of truth
   and righteousness for his name's sake (Psalm 23:3).

3. *To have direction in my life.* I want to live in the
   power and authority of God's Word every day of
   my life, and the Holy Spirit has given me God's
   promise: "I will instruct you and teach you in the
   way which you should go; I will advise you with
   My eye upon you" (Psalm 32:8 NASB). I have a
   supernatural relationship with the Word of God
   that I can't live without.

4. *To grow in my love for Jesus.* There is no other way to know the truth about Jesus Christ, the Son of God, than through God's Word. My love grows daily when I read his words, which are a direct line from his heart to mine. I'm consumed by love for him through his birth, life, death, and resurrection. John 1:1 (NIV) tells us, "In the beginning was the Word, and the Word was with God, and the Word was God," meaning Jesus.

5. *To learn to live the supernatural life as a born-again child of God.* God's Word is the light guiding me on my path in life (Psalm 119:105). The Word teaches me that the Holy Spirit lives in me (Romans 8:9) and nothing is impossible with God (Luke 1:37). God's Word tells me that I am not a weak, ineffectual person but "strong in the Lord and in the power of his might" (Ephesians 6:10).

Affirmations

- God's Word fulfills the longings of my daily life.
- I need God's Word every day.
- I receive my understanding and wisdom from the Word of God.
- The promises of God in his Word are mine.
- I have an unshakable trust in God's Word.
- I partner with the Holy Spirit in transforming my life according to God's Word.

74

THE WORD *NO*

"No weapon formed against you shall prosper, and every tongue which rises against you in judgment You shall condemn. This is the heritage of the servants of the LORD, and their righteousness is from Me," says the LORD.

ISAIAH 54:17

Meditate

When our lives are completely submitted to God and his will for us, we naturally become less attached to old negative habits that hold us down from God's best for us. We're more mindful of our behavior and attitudes. Jesus called us the light of the world (Matthew 5:14–16), and the darkness of evil in the world can't tolerate God's light. We're a threat to the darkness. The calling for the children of God is to illuminate the world with his presence. The devil and his demons can't stand that and make it their job to rob you of your light.

I want to bring your attention to God's authority and power over darkness.[13] When your identity as a child of God is solidly fixed in your head and heart, your confidence in the spiritual authority you carry increases. It only takes faith the size of a tiny mustard seed (17:20) to act on your authority. The Holy Spirit empowers the authority of God in you for you to say no to negative thinking, negative relationships, negative opinions, and negative obsessing.

---

13 See the affirmations in Meditation 47 titled "The Whole Armor of God."

Fall deeper in love with God, and your mind will open to wonderful and inspiring thoughts and choices. But how do we fall in love with God? We can't love something we don't know or aren't familiar with. Your perfect teacher is the Word of God. There's no other way to learn. Read books based on Scripture and read Scriptures itself. When you're in love with the author of all beauty, it's much easier to recognize and recoil from that which is ugly, no matter how appealing it once was to you.

Spend more time focusing your attention on the goodness of God in the world than on the evil in the world. Revelation 11:5 says God's fire will consume all that is not his. Love what is his. Say no to what's not.

Affirmations

- I say no to negative thinking and obsessing.
- I am completely submitted to God.
- I say no to all behavior that robs me of God's best.
- I say no to everything God says no to.
- I say no because I am spiritually empowered to resist what offends God.

75

I AM FORGIVING

"Whenever you stand praying, if you have anything against anyone, forgive him, that your Father in heaven may also forgive you your trespasses."

MARK 11:25

Meditate

Here's a challenge for you: for one week, set aside ten minutes a day to chronologically go back in time to forgive every person whom you've tried to forget but have not forgiven, even those offenses about which you've perhaps made the excuse that you should not have to forgive.

This exercise takes you back to your earliest days and experiences that you don't like to think about. We have all had some secret hurts, and maybe you've prayed a forgiveness prayer without being specific. Think of all the broken relationships you've pushed under the rug and not thought about for years. You may have unresolved anger stemming from earlier than grade school.

People and relationships are usually what we think about when it comes to forgiveness, but what about things out of our control, like the denominations, institutions, businesses, cities, and even countries that have hurt you? Our hearts freeze up at false accusations, discrimination, unfair regulations, fallen preachers, battling congregations, corrupt politicians, and a million other injustices and crimes and the people who commit them. Tolerance and forgiveness are not the same. The idea of "live and let live" is far from forgiveness.

Forgiveness is release. You cannot carry the weight of the wrongs you've suffered or the evils of the world. Forgiveness is not kissing evil on the cheek and saying all is well. It's giving it all, being specific, over to God, and that way you're kicking away the evil others have done to you and the evil in the world and releasing it from its stronghold over you. Unforgiveness is like gangrene in your soul; undiagnosed, it spreads through your brain and every part of you.

Don't be afraid to forgive your enemies. They won't be any less guilty. When Jesus was on earth, he offered and taught forgiveness for all of humanity. He even forgave his murderers. The only one he rejected was Satan, and you reject Satan when you release yourself from the grip of unforgiveness. These feelings rob you of blessings, healing, and even answered prayer.

Affirmations

- I keep a close watch over my heart so it won't freeze with anger that I mistake for indignation.
- I set aside my reluctance to dig deep for buried unforgiveness.
- I release the grip of unforgiveness and hidden resentment in the name of Jesus.
- I release myself from the effects of secret wounds.
- I am empowered by forgiveness.
- The Holy Spirit is teaching me how to love more and how to forgive myself.

76

I AM FORGIVEN

If we confess our sins, He is faithful and just to forgive us
our sins and to cleanse us from all unrighteousness.

1 JOHN 1:9 ESV

Meditate

What an amazing thing it is to live in the forgiving arms of
God. Isaiah 43:25 says that God blots out my transgressions
for his own sake and will not remember them. Every time I
bring up some past sin to him, he asks, *Have you forgotten?
I forgive, and it's done.*

Psalm 103:12 confirms it: "As far as the east is from
the west, so far has He removed our transgressions from
us." I'm so grateful that I don't have to carry around in my
heart and mind the things I've done in the past that I'm
ashamed of. There is nothing he won't forgive when I come
to him broken and deeply sorry for what I've done. The
weight lifted from me is miraculous. "Now in Christ Jesus
you who used to be far away have been brought near by the
blood of Christ" (Ephesians 2:13 NET). That's me. And the
same is possible for you.

So great is his love for those who fear him. It extends
as far as the east is from the west.

Affirmations

- I always ask forgiveness from God when I've sinned.
- Freedom from guilt is transforming.

- I walk in the light as he is light, and he forgives me.
- The forgiveness of God makes me more forgiving.
- God's forgiveness brings healing to my body and soul.
- I do not hesitate to ask others for forgiveness if I have done them wrong.
- God's constant forgiveness empowers me to open my eyes to see when I must ask for forgiveness from others.
- As far as the east is from the west, God has removed my sins from me.

77

ANGER

You yourselves are to put off all these: anger, wrath, malice,
blasphemy, filthy language out of your mouth.
COLOSSIANS 3:8

He would grant you, according to the riches of His glory,
to be strengthened with might through His Spirit
in the inner man.
EPHESIANS 3:16

Meditate

From a child's tearful temper tantrum to an adult's spurting
curses, anger is emotionally exhausting. Anger is the cause
of many of our physical ailments, including headaches,
high blood pressure, stroke, heart attack, skin and stomach
disorders, canker sores, and teeth and gum problems.
However you look at it, when uncontrolled, anger is a
damaging emotion.

Paul's command to the Ephesians (4:26) to "be angry,
and do not sin" can be confusing because anger is one
of the seven deadly sins. How can we not sin when we're
sinning? Also, "Do not let the sun go down on your wrath"
can confuse us because isn't wrath bad? These commands of
Paul's are warnings. If you feel anger, watch it, deal with it,
control it. Don't let the devil get hold of your anger (v. 27).
Don't let yourself be taken away with angry feelings. Deal
with the cause of those feelings right away, and whatever
you do, don't take them to bed with you. Have compassion

for yourself and tell yourself there is far more peace in you than anger.

Certain anger or indignation can be controlled and even helpful to motivate change for the better. You catch yourself in a moment of unreasonable anger, and you can make the choice to change that behavior. Righteous indignation is a call for prayer. Pray before your emotions kick in and you become trapped in them.

Affirmations

- I am not controlled by anger in any area of my life.
- I am not afraid to seek out where anger comes from in me.
- The Holy Spirit gives me self-control to drop my demands that things go right and nothing goes wrong.
- I will always make mistakes. I give myself the right to make mistakes.
- I don't go to bed harboring angry feelings.
- I don't give the devil an opportunity to get hold of the angry feelings I might express.
- I do not get angry when I make mistakes.
- I am strengthened with might through the Holy Spirit in my inner being according to the insurmountable riches of the glory of God.
- I'm free from anger's hold on me (Ephesians 3:16).

78

DISCIPLINE

Whoever loves discipline loves knowledge.
PROVERBS 12:1 ESV

I discipline my body and keep it under control.
1 CORINTHIANS 9:27 ESV

"'Those whom I love, I reprove and discipline.'"
REVELATION 3:19 ESV

Meditate

There are over fifty references to the word *discipline* in the Bible. It's not possible to live a happy and fulfilled life without discipline. We want to live lives as good people, but did you know it takes discipline to be a good person? Very few human endeavors don't require some level of discipline. Your happiness, for example, requires the discipline of teaching yourself to be happy.[14] Happiness is a skill just like patience. It takes discipline.

Keep your discipline antenna up at all times and try not to allow opportunities for operating your gift of discipline to escape you. Don't let them pass by you while you're looking the other way. From how you eat food to how punctually you arrive at events, from dwelling in depressing thoughts to thinking the thoughts Jesus thinks about you—jump in with your gift of discipline and see how much better you feel about yourself. Pampering your self-centered, I'll-do-what-I-want-and-don't-try-to-change-

14 For more information on this topic, see my book *How to Be Happy in an Unhappy World*.

me attitude never fosters a sense of well-being. It can't. Discipline and the evidence of self-control will always bring you the rewards of consistently feeling good about yourself. You can't be happy without discipline.

Affirmations

- I am disciplined in the work I do.
- I work at disciplining my emotions.
- The Holy Spirit helps me discipline the words of my mouth (Proverbs 15:1).
- An undisciplined life is an unfulfilled life.
- I am thankful the Lord shows me where I need discipline, and I immediately obey.

79

CRITICAL SPIRIT

If instead of showing love among yourselves you are always critical and catty, watch out! Beware of ruining each other.
GALATIANS 5:15 TLB

The one who guards his mouth and his tongue
keeps his life from troubles.
PROVERBS 21:23 NET

Meditate

A critical spirit is deadly. It tears apart marriages, ruins the workplace, pits friend against friend and child against parent, and causes useless battles. Criticism robs closeness from families as well as every other relationship you can name. Now is the time to remove all traces of criticism from your heart and mouth. I'm not talking about the business of critiquing, situations when we give productive responses to another's work and enjoy the same from them. I'm talking about finding fault and judging. You're too loving to allow such things to make a home in your mind and heart.

The Bible calls criticism slander (James 4:11–12). Popular humor uses criticism for laughs, but if you're the target of the jokes, it's not so funny. I have had several counseling clients with deep emotional wounds from being teased, made fun of, and criticized unfairly as children. Criticism is not the same as poking fun or teasing, but these can be equally damaging. The poke can feel more like a punch. When you're criticized, ask yourself if you aren't guilty of doing the same. We are all guilty. Think of a time in your life when you've been unjustly criticized, laughed at, teased, or bullied. Perhaps you will want to journal about how you felt.

There's nothing productive in unfair criticism. First Peter 3:10 tells us to keep our tongues from speaking evil. A good way to do that is to take a personal inventory, name any sore spots and bad habits you have, and see how critical of yourself you are. Then measure these against the words in Matthew 12:34: "Out of the abundance of the heart the mouth speaks" (ESV).

Read the affirmations that follow as permanent doors to freedom. Give yourself permission to release the love and compassion in you and stop criticizing.

Affirmations

- I refuse to tolerate a critical spirit in me.
- I will remember that my mouth speaks from my heart.
- I turn my head from all negative criticism directed at me or anyone else.
- God's love stops me from criticizing anyone or anything.
- I refuse to be affected by unjust criticism, teasing, or bullying.
- I do not place myself in situations with those who love to criticize.
- I am a loving and caring person. I choose love and compassion over faultfinding and criticism.

80

THE CONTROLLER

The LORD is my light and my salvation;
whom shall I fear?
The LORD is the strength of my life;
of whom shall I be afraid?

PSALM 27:1

Meditate

What defines a controlling person? A controlling person believes he or she has all the answers, is the only one who can get a job done right, knows what's best for everyone, and believes if he or she doesn't accomplish what's needed, it won't get done. The controller on the job creates distance and an unhappy work atmosphere because of their arrogance toward and distrust of coworkers. At home the controller makes everyone unhappy by acting as though he or she is the only one who knows how to run things and knows how things should go.

The controller may even use religious dialogue, such as, "God doesn't like what you're doing" and "God told me you should—" When we behave this way, we become the opposite of what Jesus taught about love, mercy, compassion, empathy, and kindness. If you are vexed with control issues, you may have overlooked these attributes of the Lord.

If you're stuck with a controlling person in your life, it doesn't work to fight back, argue, or point out that they are being unloving. It's not the controller you should focus on; it's you. It takes spiritual strength and patience to deal with a controller. The King James Bible refers to *patience* 34 times and the word *strong* 344 times, including "Be strong." To get out from under the power of a controller takes spiritual strength, and it includes making it clear how you feel. The controller may find it hard to listen.

If you're the controller, pay attention to what others are telling you. Agree to give them some authority and autonomy. When you begin to do this, you'll find it difficult to trust others with what you think only you can do right. You're afraid that if people don't follow your rules, principles, and orders, everything might fall apart. That's not true, of course. The urge to control others is your ego in full charge. When you follow your self-centered ego, you may behave selfishly and even manipulate others for your own gain. Positive change happens when you step out of your egotistical mindset and realize that being a controller makes everyone miserable, including yourself. Controllers aren't happy people. Open your heart to the gentler calling of the Holy Spirit to set you free.

Affirmations

- I put an end to living the life of a controller.
- I realize that love is not controlling.
- I treat others as I want to be treated (Luke 6:31).
- I listen to others when they want to voice an opinion.
- I do not have all the answers.
- Others can do my job as well as I can.
- I will not be manipulated by a controller.

81

GOD'S CALL

Jesus came and spoke to them, saying, "All authority has been given to Me in heaven and on earth. Go therefore and make disciples of all the nations, baptizing them in the name of the Father and of the Son and of the Holy Spirit, teaching them to observe all things that I have commanded you; and lo, I am with you always, even to the end of the age." Amen.
MATTHEW 28:18–20

Meditate

When you're close to God, it's normal and natural that you're touching the world with your faith in the Lord Jesus. You're walking with the light of the Holy Spirit emanating from you. Not everyone will like this light of yours, but that's all part of your calling. You're bringing the goodness of God wherever you place your feet, and that's what matters. If people reject you, just remember that rejection has nothing to do with failure. In God's kingdom, there is no failure.

Christianity has gotten a bad rap for being judgmental in the Western world over the past few years, but God continues to move in powerful ways all over the world, especially in the Southern Hemisphere. It's critical to represent the Lord and remove all rigid and judgmental attitudes. You and I aren't any better or more important than any other human on earth. Jesus died for everyone, and God sent Jesus to earth because he loves all people. God's call is to his children, who are authentic, nonjudgmental, and obedient to him. God's call is one of love.

Some Christians can get taken up with doom thinking and talking, with their focus on everything bad in the world. Others may do the opposite by denial or avoidance of evil in the world. Neither type can discern a call from God because they listen to other voices. God calls us to love the world, to have faith greater than mustard seeds, to walk in peace and joy. These are the called ones whom the Holy Spirit anoints and whom God sends into all the world.

What draws the human race more than love, truth, and acceptance? The world is desperate for Jesus, and God is calling us to care enough about his desperate world to give our lives.

Affirmations

- I am called to love God first.
- I'm called by the love of God, and it's by his love that I love and give.
- The spiritual treasure within me is more beautiful than anything I could create on my own.
- God loves to do great things through me because I love his call.
- I reach out to the whole world with my compassion.
- I fully give myself over to the Holy Spirit's methods of communicating with the people of today's world.
- "Here am I. Send me!" (Isaiah 6:8 NASB).

82

WORK

Whatever you do, work at it with all your heart, as working
for the Lord, not for human masters, since you know that
you will receive an inheritance from the Lord as a reward.
It is the Lord Christ you are serving.

<small>COLOSSIANS 3:23–24 NIV</small>

Be diligent to present yourself approved to God,
a worker who does not need to be ashamed.

<small>2 TIMOTHY 2:15</small>

Meditate

There was an artist named Bezalel living in Israel at the
time God was giving Moses explicit instructions on
the construction and design of the Lord's temple. God
detailed his instructions down to the last thread of the
priests' garments, even their underwear (Exodus 28). God
impeccably designed the temple and everything in it, and
when it came to the artist who would oversee everything,
he chose Bezalel by name. Bezalel had obviously worked
very hard to become skilled at his craft, and God filled him
with the Holy Spirit. He was a master craftsman in gold,
silver, bronze, cutting jewels for settings, carving wood,
and creating all God ordered him to do. Bezalel's job was to
make God's temple beautiful (Exodus 31:1–5).

   The work Bezalel did was no more important than
the work you do now when everything you do is for the

Lord. When the work you do is for the Lord, you'll see it as sacred, and you won't complain about it.

Imagine Bezalel alive today as a scientist, Bible teacher, pastor, nurse, Fortune 500 CEO, or waiter. Imagine what Bezalel could do with any job God gave him to do. It isn't the job that God loves but the worker who does the job and how he or she does it. Imagine Bezalel getting up in the morning and moaning, "Oh poor me. I have to go to the temple and do great skilled work again today. I don't know why God chose me for this job."

When God is our employer, we are flooded with opportunities for excellence and promotion no matter the job. We aren't born with developed skills. Bezalel wasn't born with a chisel in his hand. If Bezalel didn't really care about what he was doing or had settled for being mediocre, we would never have heard of him. Take your work as seriously as God does. Everything you set your hand to matters to the Lord.

Affirmations

- I have a warehouse of spiritual gifts.
- I appreciate and am thankful for my job.
- I bring the presence of God to my workplace.
- I am not afraid to change jobs and ask for the Lord's perfect guidance.
- I see the work I do as sacred.
- My work honors the Lord.

83

ALL THAT I DO

Whatever you do in word or deed, do all in the name of the
Lord Jesus, giving thanks to God the Father through Him.
COLOSSIANS 3:17

The purpose in a man's heart is like deep water,
but a man of understanding will draw it out.
PROVERBS 20:5 ESV

Meditate

The previous meditation focused on the work we do. Now
we look at *everything* we do. This focuses on the way we
live our lives: the roads we take, the people whose lives
we affect, the actions of our daily life. All that Jesus did as
recorded in the Bible creates a love volume of holy events.
John wrote in his gospel, "If every one of [the things that
Jesus did] were written down, I suppose that even the
whole world would not have room for the books that would
be written" (21:25 NIV). So how do we examine all we do
every day?

I suggest starting a new journal, and in it record
what you do every day but use a new way of observing.
Instead of summarizing your activities in pockets of
time like morning, afternoon, evening, and night, try
categorizing what you touched, moved, lifted, gave away.
Think of the words you've spoken or not spoken, the air
you've breathed. Instead of jotting down that you finished
some task, think about what it was you actually did,

breaking it down to its most minute details. "I picked up a book and ran my fingers on its pages. It felt good. I shivered in the cold air when I stepped outside. I liked it. I ate a frozen yogurt. I felt uncomfortable." Instead of writing, "I was on the phone for an hour," write down what you actually did on the phone for an hour. "I clicked the screen, tapped the speaker, slid the delete bar. I felt impatient." You might write down some exact words you spoke followed by what you felt. "I said, 'I look forward to seeing you too.' I felt insincere."

This isn't a journal of accomplishments, desires, dreams, hopes, worries, fears. It's a close look at how you're living your life. It will give you great insight into your relationship with God. He wants you blessed and fulfilled (Ephesians 1:3; James 1:25). Is it time to make some changes?

Affirmations

- All that I do is significant.
- All that I do is important.
- I am significant and important to God.
- The Holy Spirit illuminates my awareness of how I'm living my life.
- I refuse to miss out on the blessings God has for me.
- How I feel is an important part of all I do.
- I do good things every day to help someone.
- I give Jesus full access to my heart and all I do.

84

THE OGRES OF HURRY

Since a promise remains of entering His rest,
let us fear lest any of you seem to have come short of it.
HEBREWS 4:1

On the seventh day God ended His work which He had
done, and He rested on the seventh day from all His work
which He had done.
GENESIS 2:2

Return to your rest, O my soul,
for the LORD has dealt bountifully with you.
PSALM 116:7

Meditate

Hurry is a primary source of stress. We can be completely
caught in the cultural jaws of hurry. The very idea of
slowing down is stressful because, in our rush to produce
and achieve, we're too much in a hurry to slow down. We
live in a culture that prizes hurry. We're in a hurry to make
things happen and get things done because we fear the
opposite of hurry, which we think is being late. Wrong. The
opposite of hurry is rest.

Hurry is killing us. The Lord's admonition in Psalm
46:10, "Be still, and know that I am God," means just that.
Being still takes time and intention. Technology helps
you get things done faster, but it encourages more hurry,
not less. To get relief from the influence of hurry ogres in
the world around you and in you, consider putting your

cell phone on silent for a few moments each day to stop everything and be still and know he is God.

Our bodies, as well as our minds, beg for sacred, set-apart time to be alone and quiet with God. True rest and refreshment for our souls are found when we set ourselves apart to be alone in silence with God. You pull away not only from the busy world around you but also from the busy world within you to be alone and quiet in the presence of God.[15]

The next time you feel rushed, give yourself permission to go slower. Try walking slower and saying no to more tasks; ask yourself what's really important to you.

Affirmations

- I refuse to let the hurry of the world around me dictate my life.
- I stop myself from hurrying and ask myself what's more important to me.
- I use technology. Technology doesn't use me.
- I tell my soul to rest in the Lord.
- I'm not at war with time.
- I use my time well, and I have no need to hurry.

---

15 See Meditation 3 titled "Silence."

85

NOISE

Let it be the hidden person of the heart,
with the incorruptible beauty of a gentle and quiet spirit,
which is very precious in the sight of God.

1 PETER 3:4

After the earthquake a fire, but the LORD was not in the fire;
and after the fire a still small voice.

1 KINGS 19:12

Meditate

Did you know we can be addicted to noise? It doesn't
matter what kind of noise. We just don't want things to be
too quiet. Noise and hurry are enemies of peace. You may
believe noise is the norm, but it's scripturally abnormal.
What's normal is peace, love, and joy in the Holy Spirit.

In the midst of loud, crashing waves in a furious
storm at sea, Jesus rose up and ordered, "Peace, be still"
(Mark 4:39). Jesus didn't have a stormy soul. He didn't
confront the storm with the same fury the storm possessed.
He confronted it with who he was. He was and is peace.

With constant noise around us, there's only one way
to be heard, and that's to be noisier than the noise around
us. You've heard the expression "I can't hear myself think in
this noise." Nobody else can hear themselves think either;
noise has a way of numbing clear thinking. Suppose you
disagree with someone, and their voice rises in anger. If you
allow yourself to become loud like that person, there'll be

no resolution to the disagreement. It could go on for days, even years. Proverbs 15:1 tells us a soft voice turns away wrath, which is something we might want to tape on our refrigerators and bathroom mirrors. What if you brought forth calmness from your heart during the other person's angry outburst, and what if you showed you were listening and caring about the point they were trying to make? A storm can't calm a storm. It creates a greater storm.

Jesus transcended the storm at sea not only because he was the Son of God but also because he was peace, something he chose to be. The loud, raging storm was outside Jesus, not in him. He rebuked the storm from who he was: peace itself. The old adage "Fight fire with fire" is light-years away from what Jesus taught us. God speaks to us in a still, small voice (1 Kings 19:12), and it's difficult to hear him in storms, clamor, and relentless noise.

Affirmations

- When I am making noise, I can't hear the still, small voice of God, so I quiet myself down.
- I choose to quiet the noise in my daily life so I can enjoy God's peace that passes understanding.
- I renounce all need for noise.
- I choose to calm the noisy storms of my life with the peace of God that lives in me.
- I make a conscious effort to keep myself in a peaceful atmosphere.
- I will turn off all my audio devices for a period of time each day.

86

NEVER BORED

His compassions fail not.
They are new every morning.
LAMENTATIONS 3:22–23

He said, "Come with me,
and see my zeal for the LORD."
2 KINGS 10:16

If anyone is in Christ, he is a new creation;
old things have passed away;
behold, all things have become new.
2 CORINTHIANS 5:17

Meditate

To be bored means to be disinterested in things, people, and maybe even life itself. Boredom means you lack excitement and inspiration. As a child of God, I should never be bored because I live in the excitement of knowing God. I'm spiritually alive, and I don't depend on my natural instincts and abilities to be excited about the life I'm living. I'm continually fascinated by the presence of God everywhere I go. I discover him in the tiniest of things. I see him in the friendly nod of a stranger, in the squawk of a gull, the trace of breakfast on a baby's bib, the shine of dew on a fallen leaf. I'm fascinated by the endless opportunities to show kindness, to help someone in trouble, to create goodness where there was none.

I'm intrigued by the Word of God and how the words breathe life into every cell of me every day. There's not a moment of boredom in its teaching me, enlightening me, guiding me, challenging me, correcting me, giving me understanding in all things. Faith is always energizing, invigorating, growing, and expanding. My constant source of fascination is the love of God, which I know I can never fully comprehend in this lifetime.

Affirmations

- I am excited to be alive. Everything about me exudes life.
- I am fascinated by the world around me. I find God in all things.
- I enclose myself in the arms of God's love in order to maintain my enthusiasm for his will in the world.
- I am curious, interested, engaged, and always open to the leading of the Lord in new directions.
- I don't live for self-satisfaction.
- Boredom cannot enter the doors of my heart because I have the mind of Christ.
- I have the spiritual awareness and insight to comprehend what is the width and length and depth and height of life and to know the love of Christ, which passes knowledge (Ephesians 3:18–19).
- I am filled with all the fullness of God, and I will not be bored (Ephesians 3:19).

87

LAZINESS

The desire of the lazy man kills him,
for his hands refuse to labor.
PROVERBS 21:25

A lazy man buries his hand in the bowl,
and will not so much as bring it to his mouth again.
PROVERBS 19:24

Meditate

People often confuse fear and avoidance with laziness. Although fear can pave the way for laziness, fear doesn't produce laziness, and you don't have to be afraid in order to be lazy. The desire to do nothing produces laziness. Laziness is not avoidance behavior either. Avoidance has to do with not wanting to do something. I avoid answering a call from a bill collector because I don't want to answer it. It has nothing to do with laziness because I'm taking steps to avoid the bill collector. Laziness is being unwilling to do anything; it's refusing to act. An example of laziness is when it's the middle of February and you still haven't bothered to put away all the Christmas decorations. That's not fear, and it's not avoidance. It's laziness. You are simply unwilling to put the decorations away.

Laziness has a bad reputation because it's so unproductive. But the good thing about laziness is that it is easy to overcome. It is put to a halt with action. Boom. It's over. Unlike fear and avoidance behavior, laziness has to do with our character. With one small action, like rising up out of the chair, it's over. Once up, it's easier to stay up. You've just changed your stubborn unwillingness to being willing. Action can be a catalyst for new inner growth, greater self-awareness, and a fresher relationship with the Lord.

I must add here that rest is not laziness. If you take frequent naps, you're not being lazy. Don't confuse sleeping in on Saturday with laziness when you're tired and need the sleep. While in Quiet Prayer meditation, we're not moving around, but we are anything but lazy.[16] Rest gives you more energy, and laziness robs your energy.

Take action with lazy feelings. Move. Get up. Do the dishes. Make the bed. Fill the car with gas. Clean the bathtub. Walk. Run. Later, after you've done all you refused to do earlier, go for a walk with the Lord and release the unwillingness and resentment you've buried so well. Next time you feel lazy, remember you have the power to end it with just one action. It can be a small action. You have the Holy Spirit in you. Do it.

Affirmations

- I have a willing heart, not a lazy heart.
- Laziness will not hold me captive and rob me.
- I honor my body and mind with rest. Rest is not laziness.
- I will not be a victim of avoidance behavior or fear and call it laziness.

---

16 Quiet Prayer is the practice of being still in the presence of God. For more information on Quiet Prayer meditations, see my book *Quiet Prayer: 31 Days of Meditation for Women.*

88

THE WONDERS OF EXPLORING

The way you live will always please the Lord and honor him, so that you will always be doing good, kind things for others, while all the time you are learning to know God better and better.

COLOSSIANS 1:10 TLB

Meditate

To explore doesn't mean you have to be like Marco Polo, bringing home fabulous Chinese spices; Lewis and Clark, navigating churning rivers to map out the Louisiana territory; or my friend Phyllis, measuring the snow in Telluride. To explore can mean you look for different solutions to different problems in everyday life by considering your options for what to do, what to say, and how to understand something better.

Of course, you can always don your Ponce de León cape and head for the mysteries of San Juan, but best of all are the mysteries of the world right in front of you. You don't have to be particularly creative to ignite your inner explorer, but you do need to be curious. God gave you a wildly inventive mind to explore your world with fascination and curiosity.

King Solomon in the Bible is an example of someone with vision for exploring life. He created magnificent gardens and could speak with authority about every tree, plant, and flower he grew (1 Kings 4:33). His curiosity spanned from the cedars of Lebanon to exotic flowers and the weeds that grew in the cracks of the rocks. He explored the natural world to understand animals, birds, fish, and insects. He also created 3,000 proverbs and 1,005 songs. Curiosity leads to fascination. Fascination leads to passion.

There is more for us to explore than would fill a hundred lifetimes. It only takes looking at what's around us. My creative writing students would tell me they needed to travel and see the world in order to write about it. I told them that all they had to do to see the world was to look out their window.

Affirmations

- I am filled with holy curiosity about God's world just like Solomon.
- I ignite my desire to learn and expand my understanding of what interests me.
- I explore solutions to problems before acting on them.
- I explore the Word of God to guide me and spark my love of life.
- My love of God and life inspires me to explore the truth in everything.
- I will not quench the Holy Spirit's guidance by being rigid and opinionated and not open to learning new things.
- I am curious, fascinated, and passionate about what God will show me next.
- I can see the whole world from my window.

89

BEAUTIFUL MUSIC

It is good to give thanks to the Lord,
and to sing praises to Your name, O Most High.
Psalm 92:1

I will praise You—and Your faithfulness, O my God!
To You I will sing with the harp, O Holy One of Israel.
Psalm 71:22

Oh, sing to the Lord a new song! Sing to the Lord, all the
earth. Sing to the Lord, bless His name; proclaim the good
news of His salvation from day to day. Declare His glory
among the nations, His wonders among all peoples.
Psalm 96:1–3

Meditate

Worship music fills our souls with heaven's mind and
carries great power to move us toward a deeper connection
with heaven. Love finds us in the music we bring to the
Lord. Sing to the Lord your beautiful new song of faith and
love. Come, let's sing to the Lord. Let's worship together, for
he is our King and the ruler of all the earth. God requires
and deserves our worship, and music is a great way for us
to thank him for who he is and what he has done while
declaring his glory. Perhaps you can imagine God tapping
his toe, humming along, and enjoying us and our worship.

When in need of a divine boost of faith and energy,
sing. When in trouble, sing. When hurting, sing. When it
looks like there's no hope, sing. When you think the world

is tumbling down on you, sing. Bring brighter days to the world and sing.

Affirmations

- My life is a song to the Lord.
- I worship God.
- I sing my new song to God for all the world to hear.
- The song of love for God in me is eternal. I sing to him forever.
- My soul writes music to stir the heavens, and my heart sings music to stir the earth.
- God is the song I sing.

90

I AM CREATIVE

Whatever you do, do it heartily,
as to the Lord and not to men.
COLOSSIANS 3:23

"He has filled them with skill to do all manner of work of
the engraver and the designer and the tapestry maker, in
blue, purple, and scarlet thread, and fine linen, and of the
weaver—those who do every work and those who design
artistic works."
EXODUS 35:35

Do not neglect the gift that is in you.
1 TIMOTHY 4:14

Meditate

The creative life is an amplified life. It begins in the heart.
I believe a pure heart is the most creative because it's not
driven by ego. Competition, success, flattery, or a fear of
failure aren't the motivating forces in the creative heart.
God-given inspiration is the guiding force of all creative
endeavors. The child of God has direct access to the creative
heart and mind of almighty God for guidance.

A pure heart is a renewed heart. When God renews
and purifies your human heart, it beats with an eternal
rhythm of freedom. You're free from striving, vanity,
jealousy, competitiveness, pride, envy, greed, and self-doubt
to live creatively as he called you to live. There's no room in
your renewed heart to live a blasé or reckless life. Recognize

the difference between ambition and inspiration. They are miles apart. Only when ambition is from God is it inspired.

Everyone is creative. You are living and breathing the breath of the one who created all things. You can be creative in all things you do. You can give up trying to be clever and interesting. No need to try. You simply *are* clever and interesting. You can create an interesting environment around you because you have the creative mind of Christ.

Honor your creative self by building skills that expand your knowledge and continue to expand your world. Creativity is seeing what others want to see, and that's what God does, and so do you and I. Don't settle for a ho-hum life.

Affirmations

- Creativity is my gift from God.
- The source of my creativity is God himself.
- I am totally equipped by the Holy Spirit to turn that which was dull and boring into something illuminated.
- I'm willing to take chances and explore new things.
- I am not looking for approval.
- I am brave and do hard things.
- I am continuously inspired by the Holy Spirit.
- I am teachable and willing to work hard to develop my skills to see what God sees.

91

THE NATURAL WORLD

The heavens declare the glory of God; the sky displays his handiwork. Day after day it speaks out; night after night it reveals his greatness.

PSALM 19:1–2 NET

O LORD, how manifold are Your works! In wisdom You have made them all. The earth is full of Your possessions— this great and wide sea, in which are innumerable teeming things, living things both small and great.

PSALM 104:24–25

Meditate

God hasn't hidden himself from humanity behind scrolls on the walls of sanctuaries. His existence is plainly evident in his creation. God reveals himself in the natural world, and the natural world declares his glory. We can see his glory in every tree, shrub, blade of grass, mountain range, fjord, glacier, and anthill.

The splendor and majesty of God's creation are evident to you and me, and we've been given spiritual vision and insight into the depth of his passion for his creation. This sight inspires and makes us so much more attentive to caring for the natural world and sharing his passion.

Walk through a park, a field, the woods, or your backyard and see his glory. Whether it's a plant on a windowsill, a towering redwood, a dazzling ocean, or a puddle on the sidewalk, don't miss the wonder of it. Even in the wounds of the natural world—droughts, forest fires, floods, and pollution—we find evidence of God's glory and wisdom in all of nature. He is God of his creation.

In Solomon's famous poem in Ecclesiastes 3, he wrote of the appointed order of creation. The fourteen points of the poem begin with "To everything there is a season, and a time for every purpose under heaven" (v. 1). Every event has an appointed time under God. Notice that Solomon wrote that there's a time for everything "under heaven." All of time and creation are God's. There's an appointed time and rhythm for everything under God's heaven, from a starfish on the beach at Cancún to a rain forest in Belize. From an earthquake in Malaysia to a snowstorm in Minnesota, you and I are here and part of it all, both small and great.

Affirmations

- I thank God for such a beautiful world.
- God created the natural world as an expression of himself, and I can see his grace and beauty in everything that grows.
- I love nature, but it's God I worship.
- I am part of every purpose under heaven.
- The Holy Spirit opens my ears and eyes to God's appointed times and seasons, and I am humbled by the enormity of every purpose under heaven.
- I honor God by taking care of his natural world in every way I can.

92

ANIMALS

God made the wild animals according to their kinds, the
cattle according to their kinds, and all the creatures that
creep along the ground according to their kinds. God saw
that it was good.

GENESIS 1:25 NET

Meditate

In Genesis 1:26 God gave Adam authority over every living
thing God created on earth. Throughout the Bible we see
God's love and tenderness for the animals he created and
provided for humans to care for and use.

Animals have always played an important role in
God's kingdom on earth, from providing transportation,
food, and clothing to being sacrifices in the Israelites'
worship tradition. Household pets have provided and
continue to provide comfort, blessing, friendship, labor,
and assistance to their human caretakers. David spent many
years as a shepherd living with his flocks of sheep. Jesus
used sheep to describe us, his human children (such as
"My sheep hear My voice" in John 10:27). God used a dove
to guide Noah to dry land. At Jesus' baptism in the Jordan
River, John saw an image like a dove hovering over Jesus'
head when he came up from the water.

God's desire is to bless his children, and he does this
in countless ways, even by presenting us with a world that
includes animals from elephants to snails. From the fish
of the sea to the birds of the air, we are blessed. Even the

donkey, which is known to be rather stupid and stubborn, is a favored animal. Jesus rode a donkey into Jerusalem as if it were a heavenly chariot. Don't ever underestimate the things God might do to get our attention. He is fully aware of and cares about the littlest living thing, even an ant (Proverbs 6:6). He keeps his eye on the sparrow while watching over you.

You are his favorite creation, his joy, and his everlasting love (Jeremiah 31:3).

Affirmations

- I honor and respect all of God's creation.
- I honor and respect God's taste in creating his different animals.
- I take good care of the animals that God gives to my keeping.
- I admire God's amazing creativity in all his animals, birds, and fish.
- I love the farm animals, the chickens in their coops, the cows in their stalls, the bulls in the pastures, the ponies in the corral, the pigs, the ducks, the goats. God has made all things beautiful in their time.
- I will continue to be delighted and awed by the living creatures God has put on the earth.
- I love loving God's creatures great and small.
- Loving God's creatures helps me to love people even more.

93

GOD'S METHOD OF PROVISION

"O LORD God,…may your loyal followers rejoice
in the prosperity you give."
2 CHRONICLES 6:41 NET

Beloved, I pray that you may prosper in all things
and be in health, just as your soul prospers.
3 JOHN 1:2

Meditate

The word *prosperity* in Hebrew is *shalah*, which means "ease, security, and plenty." In my early childhood, I was surrounded by adoring and loving aunts and uncles, grandparents, and parents, and though we lived very simply, nobody acted like we lacked anything. My mother taught me there were poor people in the world, but it certainly couldn't have been us because we were happy with what we had. No one ever complained that there wasn't enough to eat or that our clothes weren't good enough or that we didn't have what everyone else had. We had plenty. When I read John's letter to his friend Gaius, "Beloved, I pray that you may prosper in all things and be in health, just as your soul prospers" (3 John 1:2), I think of the blessing it was to grow up prosperous.

I've known people who were financially wealthy, but they weren't prosperous. When I think of Paul's greeting, I imagine he's addressing his friend's soul and blessing him with a prayer for an expanded, beautiful soul. You can recognize a prosperous soul because it's the inner life of a contented, wise, loving person of peace who envies nothing, lacks nothing, is grateful, is full of joy, and is kind to all. The prosperous soul is like Paul, content with and without (Philippians 4:11). Financial wealth is wonderful only if we can live with it and without it.

The prosperous soul naturally attracts a healthy life because stress-related diseases and conditions like hatred, greed, rage, dissension, and chronic anxiety don't reach him or her. A prosperous soul isn't drawn to health-sabotaging behaviors and habits. A prosperous soul is disciplined and does good, not harm, for the body. Your soul craves prosperity, and it's a journey God wants to take you on.

Read the following affirmations slowly and then pause to allow the words to rest in your soul.

Affirmations

- God provides all my needs according to his riches in glory (Philippians 4:19).
- My soul is prospering right now by expanding in love, wisdom, and the power of God in all I think, feel, and do.
- The work I do will prosper.
- I am content with everything God gives me.
- I live in the prosperity of my soul, and I rejoice.
- I lack nothing.
- I prosper as my soul prospers.

94

GOD PROTECTS ME

I will say of the LORD, "He is my refuge and my fortress; my God, in Him I will trust." Surely He shall deliver you from the snare of the fowler and from the perilous pestilence. He shall cover you with His feathers, and under his wings you shall take refuge. His truth shall be your shield and buckler. You shall not be afraid of the terror by night, nor of the arrow that flies by day, nor of the pestilence that walks in darkness, nor of the destruction that lays wastes at noonday.

PSALM 91:2–6

Meditate

I've heard about men and women who have met nose-to-nose with wild animals like bears and wolves without harm. They each are certain they escaped by remaining calm and peacefully trusting God. God's peace and our trust are powerful shields of protection against dangerous situations. The devil can't tolerate peace. Jesus called out the word *peace* to the raging waters that threatened to drown him and his disciples. The storm obeyed (Mark 4:39). God's promises to protect us are solidly fixed in his will. He will even protect us from ourselves as well as the fears we harbor.

The secret is to quiet your body as well as your mind. You may not ever find yourself face-to-face with a wolf or bear, but you will face difficult situations in everyday life. God sends his angels to take charge over you (Psalm 91:11–12), and his Holy Spirit is your physical and emotional help.

In all things and situations, you are more than a conqueror (Romans 8:31–37).

Tell yourself the following affirmations as often as you can.

Affirmations

- The Lord is my refuge and fortress. He protects me.
- I trust in my God. His faithfulness is a shield protecting me.
- The Lord is my Savior and protection.
- I am safe and secure in the presence of God.
- When trouble comes, I cling to the Lord, who never leaves me or forsakes me.
- Surely goodness and mercy follow me all the days of my life because I live in the heart of the Lord.
- God sends angels to watch over me.
- I'm surrounded by God's protection always.

95

WISDOM AND KNOWLEDGE

The wise shall inherit glory.
PROVERBS 3:35

"I am sending you out like sheep surrounded by wolves,
so be wise as serpents and innocent as doves."
MATTHEW 10:16 NET

Your obedience is known to all and thus I rejoice over you.
But I want you to be wise in what is good and innocent in
what is evil.
ROMANS 16:19 NET

Meditate

Wisdom is the power to discern correctly—discern
between what is true and what is false. It is discreet use of
knowledge. To be wise is to use your skills for good and
to have the ability to produce good in times of trouble.
Wisdom is a way of being and acting.

Knowledge can exist without wisdom. But not the
other way around. Having knowledge is having information
about something. Wisdom is the skill of knowing how to
use, change, build on, and disperse what you know. James
1:5 says, "If any of you lacks wisdom, you should ask God,
who gives generously to all without finding fault, and it will
be given to you" (NIV).

God gives us wisdom to glorify him and to use the
knowledge we have about him. Fear of the Lord, respect for
him, is the starting place on the path to knowledge. God

can bless us with wisdom through Jesus, who is wisdom itself. His wisdom is in us and ready for us to call on it.

We gain spiritual knowledge through studying the Word. Wisdom acts upon and applies that knowledge. Knowledge sees a red light ahead, and wisdom puts on the brakes. Knowledge memorizes the Ten Commandments, and wisdom obeys them. Knowledge learns about God, and wisdom loves him.

Affirmations

- I am wise.
- The gift of wisdom is in me.
- I have the gift of knowledge in me.
- I am fully prepared for each day with the Holy Spirit's gifts of wisdom and knowledge alive and ready in me.
- The wisdom of God never fails.

96

WORDS OF WISDOM

If anyone is deficient in wisdom, he should ask God,
who gives to all generously and without reprimand,
and it will be given to him.
JAMES 1:5 NET

Wisdom will enter your heart,
and moral knowledge will be attractive to you.
PROVERBS 2:10 NET

Meditate

Have you ever considered that it takes wisdom to have
peace? Or how about gentleness, courtesy, willingness to
yield, mercy, impartiality, consideration, purity, sincerity,
and no hypocrisy? If that's you and you're filled with peace,
you're a wise person according to James 3:17. I want to
know you.

The gift of wisdom isn't a product of our IQ. It's a
spiritual gift and doesn't require a diploma. Ask the Lord to
give you wisdom, and it's yours (James 1:5). Did you know
wisdom is calling for you? Could it be wisdom yearns more
for you than you yearn for wisdom? Wisdom is calling you
from all over the place. (Read Proverbs 1:20–21.) Wisdom
from heaven, along with the other eight gifts of the Holy
Spirit mentioned in 1 Corinthians 12:1–11, are supernatural
gifts, and they can't be activated by the human realm.

How important is this gift? The gift of wisdom is
essential (Proverbs 4:7). The New English Translation says

wisdom is "supreme." The Amplified Bible reads, "Get [skillful and godly] wisdom [it is *preeminent*]!" (emphasis added).

After you ask for and receive wisdom from the Lord, what do you do with it? One, learn what the Bible tells you about God's wisdom. Two, focus on one aspect of wisdom, such as peace. Peace is the fruit of wisdom. When you face a panicky situation, pull out your gift of wisdom and tell yourself, *I am at peace.* These three words are powerful. They are Holy Spirit generated, and they are wise.

Affirmations

- The Holy Spirit has given me the gift of wisdom.
- Wisdom is essential, of supreme importance, and preeminent in my life.
- I walk in wisdom.
- I recognize wisdom when I see it in others.
- I respect wisdom's place in me.
- Wisdom calls me, and I answer.
- When my choices and behavior lack wisdom, God picks me up, and we start over.
- I choose to work on becoming wiser in all I think and do by listening closely to God's leading in his Word.
- I can call on the Lord every day for wisdom, and he always answers my call.

97

I DON'T HOLD GRUDGES

"Do not judge, and you will not be judged;
do not condemn, and you will not be condemned;
forgive, and you will be forgiven."
LUKE 6:37 NET

"If you forgive others their sins,
your heavenly Father will also forgive you."
MATTHEW 6:14 NET

If you, O LORD, were to keep track of sins, O Lord,
who could stand before you? But you are willing to forgive,
so that you might be honored.
PSALM 130:3–4 NET

Meditate

God did not design you and me to hold on to grudges. We can never be free to be happy if bitterness and resentment are festering in us, no matter how hidden the grudge may be. It ferments in your soul and becomes a toxic disease. None of us will get through life without needing to forgive someone along the way, and I think it's safe to say that all of us have not only ourselves to forgive but also things, places, animals, politicians, doctors, friends, family, employers, employees, partners, and even the weather. Some of us are mad at everything.

When King David wrote the Twenty-Third Psalm, he was being violently hounded by his own son, Absalom, who vowed to kill him and take over his father's throne. Yet

David wrote, "Surely your goodness and faithfulness will pursue me all my days, and I will live in the Lord's house for the rest of my life" (v. 6 NET). Holding a grudge is as bad as hating someone. It bears foul fruit. Release yourself from all grudges and put an end to the reasons you're using to justify your grudge. The one who is responsible for the grudge is you. You can make the choice now to rid yourself of every grudge you've ever harbored. You can forgive someone and still hold a grudge against them. When this happens, you build up a warehouse of grudges. Don't let this happen to you.

Affirmations

- God gives me the inner strength to forgive everyone who has hurt me and not to hold a grudge.
- God gives me the inner strength to forgive everything that has ever hurt me.
- I'm free from the chains of bitter feelings.
- I refuse to lose my joy by holding grudges.
- Nobody and nothing can steal my joy by bad behavior.
- I am empowered by God to bless my enemies if I have any.
- I release myself from the anguish of hatred, bitterness, and anger—the cause of so much emotional pain.
- I hold no grudges (Matthew 5:44).

98

SUFFICIENT

Not that we are sufficient of ourselves
to think of anything as being from ourselves,
but our sufficiency is from God.

2 CORINTHIANS 3:5

A thorn in the flesh was given to me, a messenger of Satan
to buffet me, lest I be exalted above measure…[The Lord]
said to me, "My grace is sufficient for you, for My strength
is made perfect in weakness."

2 CORINTHIANS 12:7, 9

Not that I speak from [any personal] need, for I have
learned to be content [and self-sufficient through Christ,
satisfied to the point where I am not disturbed or uneasy].

PHILIPPIANS 4:11 AMP

Meditate

When you, like Paul, can't pull out those thorns in your
flesh, relax. God isn't saying you should enjoy or seek
out the thorns; he is saying there's a power in you bigger
than a million thorns. The thorns aren't your focus. Turn
your attention to your sufficiency in the Lord, which is
monumental, and your thorns become almost insignificant
in comparison. You may have huge obstacles facing you
that seem impossible to overcome. God is aware of the
obstacles and says you have enough grace for absolutely any
obstacle that comes your way no matter how frightening
or intimidating. Let your faith go to work. Say yes to the

thorns. Don't give them power over you. God's grace is sufficient for everything.

Know that the thorns in your flesh aren't going to last forever. Isaiah 55:13 comforts us with these words: "Where once were thorns, fir trees will grow; where briars grew, the myrtle trees will sprout up. This miracle will make the Lord's name very great and be an everlasting sign of God's power and love" (TLB). See your thorn as a blessing and watch it disappear. You have all sufficiency in the Lord.

Affirmations

- The presence of God and his Spirit dwelling in me is sufficient for my every need.
- His grace and unmerited favor are my constant companions.
- God's grace is more than enough for me.
- Life's thorns don't discourage me.
- The Lord Jesus has opened the windows of faith for me to know his grace. That is sufficient for me.
- To know the Lord is pleased with me is all I need (Psalm 41:11) because I know the thorns of life don't last forever.

99

FALLING APART

Why are you cast down, O my soul, and why are you in
turmoil within me? Hope in God; for I shall again praise
him, my salvation.

PSALM 42:5 ESV

Meditate

Sometimes when life seems too hard to handle, it feels like
the whole world is falling apart. We complain to God, crying,
Where are you? and *How could you let this happen?* which are
questions that will never have answers that satisfy us. Maybe
you've been there. These are "the dark nights of the soul" that
Saint John of the Cross wrote of in the sixteenth century. His
spiritual anguish was not only about the world outside him
falling apart but also the world within him. He wrote of his
sorrow at feeling the loss of the presence of God. The world
falls apart without the presence of God.

That's what happens to people today in times
of turmoil and suffering. We can easily fall into a deep
personal pit of despair. At these times, the joy of the Lord
slips away from us, and we're alone in the dark night of
our soul. There is help, of course, because there is nothing
we go through that the Lord does not go through with us.
It's God alone who can reach us in our pain. When our
minds are fixed on suffering, it's not easy to hear the still,
small voice of God like Elijah in 1 Kings 19:12: "After the
earthquake a fire, but the LORD was not in the fire; and after
the fire a still small voice." But God doesn't only speak to us

in a still, small voice. He'll let loose with a shout that pierces our souls like a sharp knife. Like Elijah, we can be too wrapped up in our misery to hear him, but then his voice breaks through, and we're fortified with renewed strength, power, and faith.

I often go back to Psalm 40:2 (NIV), "He lifted me out of the slimy pit, out of the mud and mire; he set my feet on a rock and gave me a firm place to stand" because that's exactly what God does. We cry for help; he hears us and does a work inside us. The healing work of God comes from within us. Experiencing the joy of the Lord seems so far away at times, but we will be lifted above the pain and suffering by the power of his compassionate love whether we want it or not. Psalm 34:18 says, "The LORD is near to the brokenhearted and saves the crushed in spirit" (ESV). Now is the time to speak your affirmations loud and clear.

Affirmations

- Though my heart may fail, I'm still here.
- Even when I don't hear him, God is with me.
- I am strong in the Lord and in his mighty power (Ephesians 6:10) even if I don't feel it.
- Jesus, in his mercy and wisdom, gives me purpose.
- Nothing can separate me from God's love, not even when my world falls apart.
- God pulls my feet out of the slimy mud and sets me on a rock (Psalm 40:2).

100

MY ETERNAL HOME

They shall be mine, saith the LORD of hosts,
in that day when I make up my jewels.
MALACHI 3:17 KJV

"God so loved the world that He gave His only begotten
Son, that whoever believes in Him should not perish
but have everlasting life."
JOHN 3:16

Meditate

Don't lose sight of where you're heading. You're in the
world, but you're not part of it (John 17:16). When you find
yourself embroiled with the endless pressures of the world,
remember the world is not yours forever. You have another
world prepared and waiting for you. Jesus said, "There are
many dwelling places in my Father's house. Otherwise, I
would have told you, because I am going away to make
ready a place for you" (John 14:2 NET).

The real secret of life is death. Everything in life is
headed there. When we understand that this is something
glorious, we stop fearing death. We live our lives as robustly
as we can in the Lord to the finish, like Paul wrote at the
end of his life in 2 Timothy 4:7: "I have fought the good
fight, I have finished the race, I have kept the faith."

Jesus met a Samaritan woman at the well of Jacob in
John 4:13–14 and told her he had water to give her that was
so amazing she'd never thirst again. "Whoever drinks of this

water will thirst again, but whoever drinks of the water that I shall give him will never thirst." He said the water that he gives is a fountain springing up into everlasting life (v. 14). The water that he spoke of is eternal life.

Stop worrying that you may not make it to heaven. Take frequent inventory of sinful offenses you make against God. Ask forgiveness. Keep watch and love God. He forgives freely. Think again of the love and forgiveness God has for you.

Jesus promised, "I give them eternal life, and they shall never perish; neither shall anyone snatch them out of My hand" (John 10:28). You and I will never die. We change residences, but we don't die.

The following affirmations are to inspire you to toss away fear or doubt and rest in the promise of heaven's open arms to you.

Affirmations

- As a child of God, one day I'll live with him forever.
- I don't fear dying because I know who I am and where I'm going.
- I am safe in the arms of eternity and have nothing to fear.
- I was born to live forever in Christ.
- I am God's child of eternity.
- I can never fall out of God's hands.
- I thank God that this life isn't all there is.
- I choose to live my life fully giving glory to God in all I do as God's child of eternity.

See what great love the Father has lavished on us,
that we should be called children of God!
And that is what we are!

1 JOHN 3:1 NIV

ACKNOWLEDGMENTS

I have so much gratitude for the team at BroadStreet Publishing, who are such a delight to work with. Many thanks to my wonderful publisher, Carlton Garborg; to Tim Payne for his care and encouragement; and to the entire editorial team for their brilliant and thoughtful editing. I am deeply indebted to Chris Garborg and Garborg Design Works for making my books beautiful.

Huge thanks to my daughter, Christa, whose love and skill brought invaluable help to shape up the endless drafts I wrote for this book. I couldn't have finished it without her.

Thanks to my students and coaching clients for all I learn from them. Thanks to Kim Kubo and the growing community of Quiet Prayer meditators and intercessors, and I have a special note of appreciation to my readers. I love you.

ABOUT THE AUTHOR

New York Times best-selling author of over thirty published books, Marie Chapian is a well-loved spiritual leader, teacher, and counselor, touching the lives of people of all ages, cultures, and walks of life. Her books include *Angels in Our Lives, Quiet Prayer: The Hidden Purpose and Power of Christian Meditation*, and *Quiet Prayer: 31 Days of Meditation for Women*. Her previous devotional books written in the voice of the Lord continue to empower lives around the world. An accomplished artist, her paintings are seen in galleries as well as corporate and private collections. She makes her home in Southern California. Listen to Marie guide Quiet Prayer meditation on her podcast, *Quiet Prayer Christian Meditation*, at QuietPrayer.org.